IAN ALLAN TRANSPORT
LIBRARY

IAN ALLAN TRANSPORT
LIBRARY

ALAN TOWNSIN

Ian Allan
PUBLISHING

Half title:
Coventry Corporation chose bus chassis built within the city for most of its requirements, and the destination display 'Radford' on preserved 94 (GKV 94) is very apt since the Daimler works was in that district. It is a CVA6 model, with AEC 7.7-litre engine, a power unit favoured in this undertaking from the mid-1930s until 1950, when this example entered service, Metro-Cammell built the 60-seat body. *T. W. Moore*

Title page:
Derby Corporation was one of a number of municipalities to standardise on Daimler buses from the mid-1930s to the 1970s. 178 (KRC 178D) was one of ten Fleetline CRG6LX with Roe bodies to Park Royal design placed in service in November 1966 as part of a fleet purchased to replace the city's trolleybuses — note the complex overhead wiring still in place in this view taken the following March. The bus behind, 123 (KRC 123), was a CVG6 with Park Royal body dating from 1957. *T. W. Moore*

Below:
Sheffield Corporation had tended to share most of its bus orders between AEC and Leyland but three Daimler Fleetlines purchased in 1962 were followed by larger batches from 1964, the two buses nearest the camera in this scene of November 1971 being from a fleet of 35 with Park Royal bodywork supplied that year. 990 is followed by 975. *T. W. Moore*

Front cover:
W. Gash & Sons of Newark proved to be a late stronghold of the Daimler CVD6 model with Daimler-built CD6 engine. The chassis of DD2 (KAL 579) had entered service with the fleet in December 1948 and was still at work on school duty over 28 years later when seen in April 1977, although the Massey body shown had replaced the Strachans original in 1958. *T. W. Moore*

First published 2000

ISBN 0 7110 2718 8

© Ian Allan Publishing Ltd 2000

Published by Ian Allan Publishing

an imprint of Ian Allan Publishing Ltd, Terminal House, Shepperton, Surrey TW17 8AS.

Printed by Ian Allan Printing Ltd, Riverdene Business Park, Hersham, Surrey KT12 4RG.

Code: 0007/B

Back cover, upper:
The Coventry municipal bus fleet and production of Daimler buses in the city were both almost at an end when this photograph of two of the undertaking's Fleetline buses was taken in Trinity Street in July 1973. The bus at the kerb, 7 (CKV 7D), dated from 1966, while 106 (YVC 106K) was almost new; both vehicles had bodywork to East Lancs design, although that on No 7 was actually built by Neepsend of Sheffield. *T. W. Moore*

Back cover, lower:
The CB was in production for the Army from soon after the outbreak of war in August 1914, and even those built for civilian use tended to take on a rather military look with features such as the towing hooks and crash-bar in front of the radiator. This example was in use as a coal lorry. *MBRT*

Contents

Acknowledgements

Daimlers were prominent among the buses in which I rode to school from 1936, and early curiosity led me to study information from a multitude of sources. Contact with Daimler itself began in my days in the trade press in the 1960s, by which stage the company had become a Jaguar subsidiary, and my thoughts go back to Andrew Whyte, then Press Officer, and best known as an authority on all things Jaguar, but just as friendly and efficient if I fired him a question on some obscure bus matter. Before his untimely death, he and I discussed co-operating on a Daimler history, with my help on the bus side, and I am sure he would have enjoyed expanding studies he had already made, no doubt with strong emphasis on the people involved, just as he had in regard to Jaguar. Certainly I have been conscious of his approach in writing this volume, and hope he would have approved.

Within Daimler itself my contact was mainly with Bob Crouch, then Daimler's Bus Sales Manager, who had joined the firm as an apprentice in 1932. He too was someone who saw life as a matter of building bridges, with strong benefit to the company he served.

I am especially grateful to Phil Groves, Gavin Martin and Brian Thackray, who read the draft text with the benefit of their own knowledge from varying viewpoints. All contributed valuable additional information, some leading to fresh lines of discovery on events of 70 years or so ago.

Books concentrating on the car side of the Daimler story, notably *The Daimler Tradition* by Brian E. Smith and *Daimler Century* by Lord Montagu and David Burgess-Wise, have been useful sources of reference, mainly in regard to the company's complex early history. With regard to early buses, the writings of Charles E. Lee and a booklet *Daimler and Benz and their Influence on the Automotive Industry in Great Britain* issued in 1961 by Daimler-Benz AG helped spell out the true story.

Many of the illustrations, including quite a number originally issued by Daimler for publicity purposes, are drawn from the Ian Allan Library (IAL), the collection of T. W. Moore (TWMC), Tom Moore's own photography (TWM), the Museum of British Road Transport's archive collection in Coventry (MBRT) or my own collection (AATC). Other pictures are acknowledged individually, although I should like to thank the Omnibus Society and the Imperial War Museum for their co-operation, and G. H. F. Atkins for making some particularly interesting examples of his work available for inclusion.

Introduction

Generally, British bus builders lived in a separate world from the car makers but Daimler was 'different' in not only sharing a famous name going back to the roots of the motor car but one associated with the top of the social scale. Considered in a more practical way, the story of Daimler buses rests on a series of engineering choices and commercial alliances. Despite its top-drawer image, the firm was by no means always well led and was often short of funds to develop its ideas thoroughly; inevitably this influenced the course of events, sometimes in ways which later proved unexpectedly beneficial.

The sleeve-valve engine brought early success for buses so powered from 1912, but then came a change of course as the first of a series of links with AEC came into effect, with joint involvement in the large-scale manufacture of Army lorries for World War 1. That agreement with AEC lapsed, but was revived in a more formal form in 1926 when buses and lorries were sold under the Associated Daimler name, only to fall apart again after two years.

Far more durable was the inspired marriage of the fluid flywheel with the Wilson epicyclic gearbox introduced in 1930, which was to remain a key feature of almost all Daimler buses thereafter, as well as being made available to AEC. It was perhaps the firm's most important achievement, particularly well suited to city bus work and pointing the way to the automatic transmission taken for granted for such duty nowadays. By then Daimler's bus engines were not a strong point, but the demand for the greater economy of diesel power led to a step no doubt seen as a stop-gap choice — the adoption of the bought-in Gardner engine. As it turned out, this was soon to be recognised across the industry as a bench-mark for efficiency. From 1934, the resulting COG5 model with the five-cylinder Gardner 5LW engine was attracting major orders from municipalities, most notably Birmingham.

After World War 2 this pattern continued and, although Daimler by then offered its own diesel engine in the CVD6 chassis, the Gardner was still the more popular choice for double-deckers — by then mainly the six-cylinder CVG6 model — with strong successes until the later 1950s, when the firm was hit by falling demand for both cars and buses. In 1960, Daimler was taken over by Jaguar, which saved the bus side of the business from probable extinction by backing a project for a rear-engined double-decker, the Fleetline. Here again, the Gardner engine played a big part in the unprecedented level of sales success, extending beyond Daimler's traditional municipal strongholds to include many BET and Scottish company fleets, with London Transport as the biggest customer of all for the type, in the 1970s.

In 1968 Daimler was taken into the giant but inherently flawed British Leyland combine — in the long term this was to prove the kiss of death for the bus side of Daimler, just as it was for AEC; eventually even Leyland itself was to suffer disastrously. Bus production at Daimler's Coventry works ended in 1973, although the Fleetline continued to be built at Leyland until 1980. There had been failures as well as successes — and even the Fleetline, like other early rear-engined models, was by no means trouble-free — but the upheavals in both the manufacturing and operating sides of the industry tended to paralyse much-needed design changes which could have put that right. The story of Daimler was long and complex and its contribution to the British bus scene is rather apt to be overlooked, yet it is far too important to pass unrecognised, a task this volume seeks to address.

Alan Townsin
Steventon, Hants
January 2000

Left:
New Street, Birmingham, was a sure bet for an almost continuous parade of Daimler buses at any date from 1935 until only a few years ago. This October 1975 scene in West Midlands PTE days is composed mainly of Fleetlines, the first bus being one of the first 100 with Park Royal bodywork delivered new to the PTE, followed by a 1964 example that had been new to Birmingham Corporation, but also bodied by Park Royal. Further back, among more Fleetlines, an ex-Birmingham 'standard' can be seen. *T. W. Moore*

1. In at the Beginning

The Daimler name is apt to be considered as very 'British' within this country, thanks to the products of the Coventry-based firm bearing it, probably most associated in the public mind with limousines and up-market cars, although also familiar for many years on the buses which are the main subject of this book. Yet the name comes from Germany, going back to the very roots of the motor vehicle and the internal combustion engine, even though the direct link of the British Daimler concern with its origins barely survived into the 20th century.

Gottlieb Wilhelm Daimler, the son of a baker, was born in the village of Schorndorf, in Wurttemburg, in 1834. Mechanically-minded from the start, by 1872 he was at the Deutz gas engine works, helping Nicolaus Otto to develop his ideas on the four-stroke engine (which is still the basis of most vehicle power units), and being joined by Wilhelm Maybach, who became a lifelong friend.

In 1882, Daimler and Maybach began work independently at Cannstatt, near Stuttgart. An engine was developed in 1883 and what is claimed as the first motor-cycle was running in 1885. Another pioneer, Carl Benz, working quite separately, developed a three-wheeled car using an engine of his own design at his Mannheim works that same year, but Daimler converted a horse-drawn carriage in 1886. A second Daimler four-wheeled car, built from scratch to be motor-driven, was built in 1889 and Daimler Motoren Gesellschaft was founded in 1890.

A major objective was to expand the business by exploiting Daimler engine patents internationally. Frederick Richard Simms, a member of a Warwickshire family though born in Hamburg, met Daimler as a fellow exhibitor at an exhibition in Bremen in 1890. A friendship developed and Simms purchased the Daimler engine patent rights for the United Kingdom and its colonies. He founded the Daimler Motor Syndicate Ltd in 1893, using a rented railway arch near Putney Bridge, London — engines for boats on the Thames were initially the main line of business. However, initial steps were taken in 1895 to float a company to make vehicles using Daimler patents in Britain, even though at that date progress in this country was severely restricted by the Locomotives on Highways Act limiting speed to 4mph, with a man walking ahead.

Meanwhile, progress in Europe was rapid, Daimler engine patents being taken up vigorously in France, notably by Panhard & Levassor, which introduced the concept of putting the engine at the front of the vehicle. At that point, there was a huge expansion of interest in the potential of motor vehicles, and Harry John Lawson, already a rich man on the basis of interests in the bicycle business centred on Coventry, stepped in, offering Simms a large sum for the Daimler patents. The outcome was that it was he who floated the Daimler Motor Co Ltd in 1896, the directors mainly being Lawson's business associates. Simms was not on the board but was retained as Consulting Engineer, and J. S. Critchley was appointed as Works Manager; such practical progress as was made seems to have been due mainly to the efforts of these two.

Pressure for relaxation of the law on use of self-propelled vehicles was rising, and it was helpful that the then Prince of Wales (later to become King Edward VII) expressed interest, being taken for a short drive in a Cannstatt-built Daimler owned by F. R. Simms in February 1896 — the beginning of a long association with the Royal family. This and other publicity encouraged the Daimler Motor Co Ltd to acquire a former cotton mill in Coventry for use as its factory in April 1896. The repeal of the Locomotives on Highways Act followed later that year, opening up huge possibilities. Lawson, aiming at a monopoly, had also set up the Great Horseless Carriage Co Ltd and a major part of the factory was sold to this concern, which in 1897 became the Motor Manufacturing Co, its vehicles being known as MMC.

The weaknesses of the Daimler company in terms of manufacturing methods then became evident — for a time, cars, engines or parts were

Left:
This 1897 wagonette was an early product of the Daimler Motor Co Ltd from its Coventry factory — similar tiller-steered chassis were used for cars and a van version was also offered. Similar-looking but slightly larger Daimler wagonettes were used for several pioneer bus services. *MBRT*

imported. There were plenty of orders and there was access to German and French designs — early examples, Britain's first production cars, were virtually copies of Panhard models and crude in execution by comparison with what was to follow a few years later; deliveries of Coventry-built cars did not begin until late 1897, and then only fitfully. A small 4hp parcel van of Panhard design was among the initial range of models and has some claim to be regarded as the first British commercial vehicle offered for general sale.

There were pioneer ventures involving small open buses — in those days called motor wagonettes — in various parts of Britain in the period from 1897 to 1903, several involving vehicles described as Daimlers or having Daimler engines. MMC was importing Panhard engines to German Daimler design, and its wagonettes were also chosen. The Daimler patents meant that the name was applied widely — for a while it was apt to be used much as Hoover is nowadays applied to vacuum cleaners.

A chassis of German Daimler design, with snub-nosed bonnet, was used in an extraordinary prototype bus assembled in Bristol by Brazil, Holberrow & Straker — the last-mentioned name being that of Sidney Straker, a consulting engineer and prominent pioneer — in 1898. It had a basically single-deck body with Continental-style open rear platform but with a single forward-facing row of seats on the roof at the front, above and behind the driver, and is said to have run in London. However, in October 1899 it was a pair of similar-looking German-built Daimler chassis with 12hp four-cylinder petrol engines and standard London-style 26-seat double-deck horsebus bodies, again reputedly a Straker design, but operated by a company called the Motor Traction Co Ltd, that established the future pattern of motorbus design for operation in London. The service ran between Kennington and Victoria station, but ceased in 1900.

That same year, a new and more powerful car had been developed for the British Daimler concern by Sidney Straker, by then acting as that company's Consulting Engineer. (He was later to set up Straker-Squire, importing Büssing chassis from Germany and later making its own vehicles.) This used a 20hp four-cylinder engine based

on a Maybach design, and provided the basis for a larger chassis to carry a 10-seat open wagonette body. Two such vehicles, as well as some of MMC manufacture, were operated in London on a route between Streatham and Clapham Junction inaugurated on 1 April 1901 by a firm managed by Walter Flexman French, who was later a key figure in establishing Maidstone & District and other major bus-operating companies in southeast England. The service lasted only a few months due to very heavy maintenance and repair costs; everyone was learning the hard way about suitable materials and lubrication — rear tyres would last a day and brass gearbox bearings only a week.

Meanwhile, in 1899, Simms had resigned as Consulting Engineer to the Coventry Daimler concern, tending to revert to closer association with the German firm. However, he commissioned a Coventry-built Daimler chassis, with a German Daimler 3.3-litre four-cylinder engine, for what he called a 'War Car' — in effect a large, rather boat-like armoured car — fitted with Vickers armour-plating and two machine guns, measuring 28ft long and 8ft wide. It was not completed until April 1902, and by then the Boer War, for which it had been intended, was almost over and the project was abandoned, but it was a remarkably advanced concept. Gottlieb Daimler had also resigned from his nominal directorship of the British Daimler concern in 1899 — his health was failing and he died in March 1900, not living to see the full fruits of his pioneer work.

It so happened that, shortly afterwards, Maybach had designed a car with new and advanced features made by Daimler Motoren Gesellschaft to the order of an Austrian banker, Emil Jellinek, who entered it in races early in 1901 using the name of his daughter, Mercedes. It was very successful and the name was henceforth adopted for the firm's cars. (The Mercedes-Benz title did not arise until a merger with the Benz concern created the Daimler-Benz combine in 1926.)

A 2-ton lorry had been developed in Gottlieb Daimler's time in 1898; it had a front-mounted two-cylinder engine and what was called pinion drive, with small gears engaging internally-toothed rings in the rear wheels — a form of drive much favoured on the German Daimler lorry and bus

Right:
The Daimler Motoren Gesellschaft based at Cannstatt introduced this 2-ton lorry in 1898 — the basic family resemblances in the products of the German and British Daimler concerns were still quite strong at that stage, and both firms had graduated to using a steering wheel. This model used a two-cylinder engine known as the Phoenix, using Bosch electrical ignition instead of the glow-tube system favoured earlier. It also had 'pinion drive', to be favoured for German-built Daimler commercial vehicles for a decade or so. *AATC*

Above:
Milnes-Daimler buses used chassis imported from the German Daimler company's works at Marienfelde, most having bodywork by G. F. Milnes & Co. Among the earliest were a pair of 16hp models placed in service in May 1903 by the Lynton & Barnstaple Railway but purchased by the Great Western Railway and operated in Cornwall from Helston station to The Lizard from August that year, as seen here. They took GWR numbers 1 and 2, becoming AF 37 and AF 36 under the registration system that began that year. *AATC*

Below:
Milnes-Daimler's 24hp model with double-deck bodywork, introduced in 1904, had a radiator style not unlike that of Mercedes cars of the period. The then new London Motor Omnibus Co Ltd, which used the fleetname 'Vanguard' and later became the Vanguard Motorbus Co Ltd, was sufficiently impressed to secure a prior call on output, building up a large fleet in 1905-8, before being taken over by the LGOC. The former Vanguard works at Walthamstow was to play a fresh part in the Daimler story from 1913, as explained in the next chapter. *AATC*

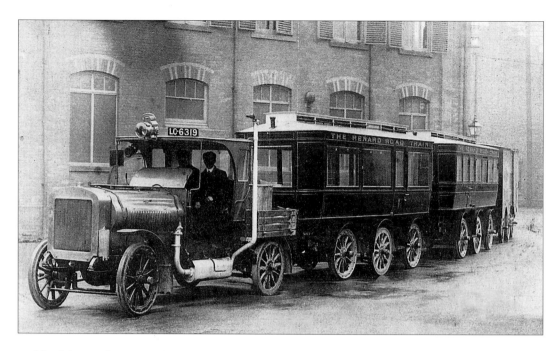

models of the next few years rather than the chain drive widely favoured by other makers. In principle it was effective but, as the gearing was exposed, road grit soon made it noisy.

In 1899 a separate concern, Motorfahrzeug und Motorenfabrik Berlin AG, based at Marienfelde, Berlin, was set up to build commercial vehicles including slightly larger four-cylinder models, these being briefly known as Marienfelde or MMB, although this company was absorbed back into Daimler Motoren Gesellschaft in 1902; later commercial vehicles built there were generally called Daimler Marienfelde until 1914. It seems that some commercial vehicle work continued for a time at Cannstatt, for what was described as a Cannstatt-Daimler was used by none other than Henry John Lawson as the basis for what was claimed to be the first large bus on rubber tyres (solid, at that date), placed in service by C. C. Dennis on a Lewisham-Eltham route in October 1902 and running until early 1904. This had an earlier style of chassis than was then being built at Marienfelde, with driver positioned quite high and over the engine; the horsebus-style double-deck body seated 27.

In 1901, G. F. Milnes & Co Ltd, of Hadley, near Wellington, Shropshire, then one of the main builders of electric tramcars in Britain, had begun marketing a 2-ton motor lorry (initially under its own name) which was actually an imported Marienfelde, and Milnes, advised by F. R. Simms, secured the sole agency for this make. From late 1902, this was succeeded by a new agreement under which the German Daimler company would supply chassis from the works at Marienfelde to a new company, Milnes-Daimler Ltd, incorporated on 27 November 1902, with its address at Hadley. At about the same time, the emphasis switched to buses, for which the Milnes factory was to supply the bodywork. Whether there was any form of understanding that dissuaded the Coventry-based Daimler concern from engaging in commercial vehicle construction has not come to light, but, whatever the reason, there was no progress in that direction for several years.

By contrast, the Milnes link with German-built Daimler chassis proved to be very effective, the design being among the more reliable of the period, except for the final-drive noise problem; it doubtless helped that Milnes was already very well known in British transport circles. Eastbourne Corporation broke new ground by beginning a motorbus service using four Milnes-Daimler 16hp single-deckers on 12 April 1903. The Great Western Railway opened a service between Helston and The Lizard with 22-seat buses of similar type in August (the first pair already briefly operated by the Lynton & Barnstaple Railway from May); it was to build up a fleet of 108 Milnes-Daimler buses by 1908.

In February 1904, a new 24hp double-deck model was added, opening up a wider market — there were only 20 motorbuses at work in London at the beginning of 1905, but five were Milnes-Daimler double-deckers, a pointer to the role the marque would play in the rapid expansion that followed. By March the first five of a fleet of such buses began work for the recently-established London Motor Omnibus Co Ltd, using the fleetname 'Vanguard'. The London General Omnibus Co also took delivery of its first of this make in May, but Vanguard secured a prior call on output. By 1907 there were some 600 Milnes-Daimler buses in service in Britain, making it by far the largest supplier, although in July 1908 a merger brought Vanguard and another major fleet into LGOC ownership, and a subsequent decision by that concern to make its own buses cut the size of the potential market quite sharply. By that date, there were over 1,000 motorbuses operating in London, of which 312 were Milnes-Daimlers, but competition was already growing and the golden days for the firm died

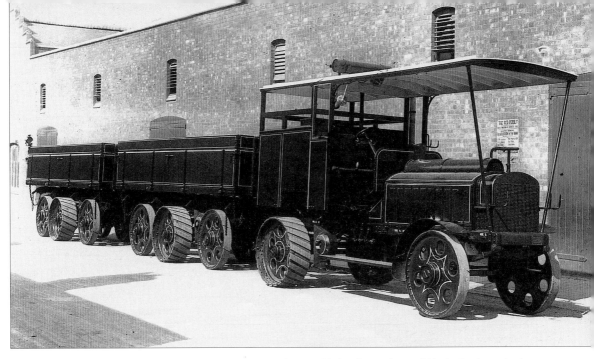

Left:
Daimler took up the manufacturing rights of the Renard Road Train as being built in Paris, this example with London registration LC 6319 and enclosed trailers being said to have taken part in the Lady Godiva procession in Coventry in August 1907. *MBRT*

Above:
Later Coventry-built Daimler Road Trains were of heavier-duty construction, using traction engine technology, though with a substantial bonnet housing a petrol engine of up to 16-litre capacity. The drive was shared between the rear wheels of the tractor and the centre pairs of wheels of the trailers, this accounting for their increased width and the diagonal strakes fitted to minimise slip on soft ground. The front and rear wheels of the trailers were steered from the drawbar linkage. *MBRT*

Below:
The British Daimler company's first venture into relatively orthodox full-sized buses came as the result of a venture for indirect involvement in the fast-expanding business of bus operation in London. The chassis of this vehicle is similar to that of a prototype double-decker exhibited at a commercial vehicle show held at Olympia in March 1908 in having the rear of the body supported on springs from the unsprung rear of the chassis; like that vehicle, it may have had electric transmission of Auto-Mixte origin. The open-sided body was evidently intended for excursion use. *TWMC*

The 1908 Show vehicle, DU 304, was looking a little shabby when posed alongside the KPL prototype bus, registered DU 1251, probably for the public announcement of the latter model in June 1910. The earlier vehicle, seen with the double-deck body intended for London service with the Gearless Omnibus Co Ltd whose name it bore on the sides, had proved to be too heavy to comply with a newly-introduced 3½-ton weight limit. That acted as the signal for the design of the KPL, which bristled with new ideas. *TWMC*

away. The emphasis switched to Mercedes car imports, but the 1914–18 war with Germany put a stop to that too, and the business was wound up in 1916.

Meanwhile, at Coventry, Daimler had passed through further difficult times in the first years of the century, narrowly avoiding bankruptcy and losing J. S. Critchley, who advised the British Electric Traction Co on its early bus ventures before designing the first car to be built by Crossley Bros. Reconstruction as The Daimler Motor Co (1904) Ltd, with fresh capital and more competent management, put the business on a firmer footing. In 1905 MMC was in receivership, and Daimler was able to reoccupy a four-storey building on the site, which had become known as the Motor Mills, as well as building new machine and erecting shops. A major figure in the story was Percy Martin, an American engineer born in Columbus, Ohio, in 1871, who joined Daimler in 1901, initially to replace Critchley as Works Manager, becoming Manag-

ing Director in 1906. He was to remain with the company until 1934, latterly as Chairman.

Charles Yale Knight, born in Salem, Indiana, but working as a journalist in Wisconsin, had become interested in reducing engine noise, notably from the mechanism used to operate the conventional type of valves, called poppet valves, held shut by a strong spring and opened at the required stages as the engine turns to allow the air/fuel mixture into the cylinder through the inlet valve, or the burnt gases out through the exhaust valve. To allow for expansion, a small amount of clearance ensures that the valves remain firmly shut during the compression and combustion stages of the sequence of operation. On early engines there was quite a sharp impact as the cam closed this gap, accounting for much of the mechanical noise emitted.

The key feature of Knight's mechanism was that the function of the valves in admitting and exhausting gases was provided by openings cut into slim sleeves surrounding the piston, which were moved smoothly by an eccentric mechanism in a manner then familiar on steam engine valvegear. The Knight design used two sleeves per cylinder, one inside the other. A quieter engine duly resulted, and 'Silent Knight' made a good trade name. Knight built a car with a prototype engine in 1905, but was finding it difficult to find licencees; in a reversal of the common flow of talent westwards across the Atlantic, he brought it to England in response to a request from Edward Manville,

Daimler's Chairman. On 1 April 1908 Daimler acquired the patent rights for Britain.

Frederick William Lanchester, the son of an architect, and by then consultant on engineering matters to the Daimler company, was given the task of developing the Knight engine, which evidently was in need of extensive redesign. Lanchester was the eldest of three brothers and, also dissatisfied with the standard of refinement of early cars, had begun work on his own design in 1894. The unusual vehicle that resulted, with engine mounted centrally behind the front seats and using worm drive for the rear axle in the quest for quietness, was put into production in 1901, but, as with Daimler, the Lanchester company was let down by poor management by its financial backers and went into receivership in 1904. Although the firm recovered, Frederick Lanchester was no longer involved in its management, leaving him free to work for Daimler, where he was to have considerable influence.

Two ventures into larger commercial vehicles came into the public eye in 1908. One was the purchase of the manufacturing rights of the Renard Road Train, developed by Colonel Renard and built in Paris from 1903, initially using a Darracq engine. It comprised a four-wheel tractor from which a universally-jointed shaft was extended through a series of three or four six-wheeled trailers, driving the centre pair of wheels on each, the front and rear wheels being steered by linkage to follow the tractor. The basic problem was that the multiple universal joints of the type then available became very noisy when operating at an angle. Even so, several examples were built by Daimler, later examples having a 16-litre engine and mostly being exported — one sent to India was used to carry cotton and marble, and another in Australia was found in derelict form in the 1970s.

The other venture made public in March 1908 was a Daimler double-deck bus, displayed at a commercial vehicle show held at Olympia, London. It was the result of a plan for Daimler involvement in bus operation in London, in which the first step had been the incorporation of the Gearless Motor Omnibus Co Ltd, headed by Edward Manville, in 1906, the name arising from the exclusive rights to use an electric transmission system developed by Henri Pieper of Liège. The principle was derived from an American Fischer design, in that case using a petrol engine and dynamo to charge batteries which then drove

the vehicle by an electric motor; one such bus had been tried by the LGOC in 1903 but rejected because of its weight. It was envisaged that Gearless would operate 150 buses using the Pieper system. There had been plans to begin by importing vehicles from Belgium, but it was then decided that Daimler should build them.

Outwardly the resulting prototype bus was of relatively conventional design for the period, with bonneted layout; it was notable in having an example of the finned style of radiator, then newly introduced on Daimler cars and not generally adopted for Daimler buses until much later. It had a 30hp four-cylinder engine, and the Auto-Mixte electric transmission was the product of a Pieper subsidiary. It used a regenerative principle, the engine-driven dynamo-tor charging batteries when running under easy conditions. For starting or under heavy load, the batteries assisted the engine by driving the dynamotor as a motor. Another unorthodox feature was the lack of conventional rear springs, although the body, pivoted to the chassis frame at the front, was supported by springs at the rear. It was registered in Coventry as DU 304 but remained unique, falling foul of revised Metropolitan Police regulations of August 1909 limiting unladen weight to 3 tons 10cwt.

By 1909, Daimler-Knight sleeve-valve engines had gone into production, the first two being four-cylinder units rated at 22 and 33hp, of 3.76- and 6.28-litre capacity. A six-cylinder version of the latter engine, with 9.4-litre capacity, was also added to the range that year, and King George V took delivery of two 57hp cars with this engine the following year. A wide range of engines was produced, from 1.7 litres upwards, but at that stage all were designed for use in private cars. By 1910 Daimler had become a well-respected motor manufacturer employing 3,000 people on night as well as day shifts to meet the demand for its cars.

Forced to go back to the drawing board with its bus project, the Daimler management put Frederick Lanchester in charge and allowed him a 'clean piece of paper' approach. The result, revealed in June 1910, was a remarkably advanced vehicle, known as the KPL from the initials of the patentees of some of its features — **K**night sleeve-valve engine, **P**ieper electrical transmission and **L**anchester worm drive. It is thought to have been the first example of what could be described as integral construction applied to a bus, using a trough-shaped sheet-steel underframe to which the mechanical units and steel-framed body structure were directly attached. There was an echo of

Lanchester car practice in the lack of a bonnet at the front, due to the use of a mid-engined layout.

However, the bus had two engines, each a four-cylinder unit rated at 12hp, mounted one on each side together with a Pieper-system dynamotor, with the drive taken through a propeller shaft to separate Lanchester worm drive units on each side of the rear axle. There were magnetic clutches for each engine, and magnetic braking was also a feature, in addition to conventional brakes on front as well as rear wheels — braking of the front wheels would not become common practice until the mid-1920s. Special wheels, of 48in diameter at the rear and 40in at the front, were constructed by Rudge-Whitworth, creating possibly the only wire-wheeled double-deck design.

Two prototypes are known to have been built, one, registered DU 1251, receiving several modifications before being operated experimentally in Birmingham for about a month in December 1911 by the Birmingham & Midland Motor Omnibus Co Ltd (better known as Midland Red), which had run 15 Milnes-Daimlers in 1904-7. Further progress with the KPL was to be halted by difficulty over a patent, turning Daimler bus development in a quite different direction.

Left:
Photographic evidence shows that DU 1251 was the subject of several design changes, the precise sequence of which is not known. The most remarkable, seen here in Moor Street, Coventry, was this covered-top version, looking distinctly top-heavy despite the lack of upper-deck glazing; the front 'windows' were covered in wire-mesh. However, it was tilt-tested in this form, though possibly without passenger loading. *TWMC*

Above:
This view in the spacious main erecting shop in Radford works, then recently built, confirms that two KPL buses were in simultaneous existence at one stage, being visible on the left of the picture. The leading vehicle appears to be DU 1251, in the form in which it was demonstrated to Midland Red in late 1911, with rear mudguard modified from that shown in the main side view — the dusty look suggests the photograph may have been taken some while after that event, by which time the project was doubtless regarded as abandoned, as explained in the next chapter. The second vehicle, with conventional exposed radiator, may have been a works 'hack', used for development. *MBRT*

2. New Alliances

The Birmingham Small Arms Co (BSA) had been formed in 1861 as an amalgamation of 14 gunsmiths in the city. In 1881 it added bicycles and parts for them to its products, and in 1910 BSA's Deputy Chairman, Dudley Docker, advocated the acquisition of a substantial car business. The choice fell on Daimler, and the deal was accepted by Daimler shareholders that October. The firm was reconstituted as The Daimler Co Ltd, with four BSA and three of the former Daimler directors.

Early in 1911, there was a resurgence of interest in the possibilities of large-scale bus operation in London, heightened by the appearance of the London General

Below:
In contrast to the KPL, the CC of 1912 represented well-tried orthodoxy, with a strong resemblance to the London General Omnibus Co's B-type as built from 1910. This was hardly surprising as Frank Searle, the latter's designer, had joined Daimler to build it. The style of radiator, with central 'hump', established a long-lived pattern, but the six-spoke front wheels were peculiar to this family of pre-1914 Daimlers. This was an early example of the fleet built for the oddly-named Tramways (MET) Omnibus Co Ltd which began entering service in January 1913, triggering the first chapter of a link with AEC. *TWMC*

Omnibus Co's new standard B-type bus the previous autumn and general recognition of its potential. By March 1911, 250 had been built, and chassis output at the LGOC works at Walthamstow, on the eastern outskirts of London, was being stepped up. Daimler, now with BSA behind it, proposed to set up the Premier Motorbus Co Ltd to operate buses in London, and Frank Searle, the LGOC's Chief Motor Engineer and architect of the B-type, was approached to become its General Manager. Although Searle did not commit himself at that stage, the plan became public knowledge; he was interviewed by LGOC's board on 4 May 1911 and offered a five-year contract to stay, but his unwillingness to commit himself there and then led to his appointment being terminated.

A plan of action to counter what was seen as a threat to existing bus operators in London had been set up for the meeting; it was also attended by two directors of Thomas Tilling Ltd, long-term rivals of the LGOC but already co-operating to a limited extent. They told LGOC of an approach from Daimler to purchase the patent rights to the petrol-electric system developed by Tilling's motor engineer, Percy Frost-Smith, and others in 1907 (and as used in Tilling-Stevens buses until the mid-1920s), of which

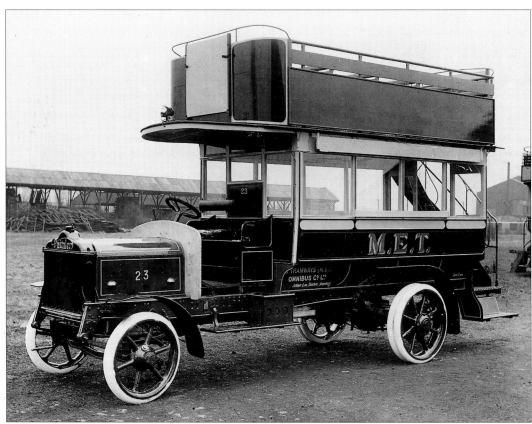

Tilling held an option to buy the rights for £3,000. The Daimler Co had offered to buy the rights for £5,000, in effect conceding that the KPL bus was vulnerable to patent challenge in this regard. Instead, Tilling and the LGOC entered into a complex deal, whereby, if a legal action to challenge the Pieper patent succeeded, the existing limited degree of joint working between LGOC and Tilling would be extended somewhat. The patent infringement was upheld and the Premier project abandoned. More significantly, in relation to the history of bus design, the entire KPL project was abandoned.

However, Searle had joined Daimler to inaugurate a commercial vehicle department. A new design of double-deck bus, Type CC, evolved, reverting to orthodox general design, including the gearbox, with strong general and detail resemblances to his B-type design for the LGOC and suitable for a similar 34-seat body of the open-top, open-staircase type then the norm. Its key feature was the use of a Daimler sleeve-valve engine, this being a four-cylinder unit of 110mm bore, 150mm stroke and 5.7-litre capacity called the '40hp', although its rating under the RAC system derived from the bore size was 30hp and the model was sometimes known as the 'CC30'. The radiator had the name 'Daimler' in script lettering cast quite boldly into the face of the top tank, which had a distinctive hump under the filler cap; this general style was to remain standard for Daimler commercial vehicles until the mid-1920s.

Above:
Daimler soon established sales of buses to municipalities as an important part of its business — a characteristic that was to persist to the end of production. This one was Sheffield Corporation's first motorbus, No 1, registered W 3201, which entered service on the Lodge Moor route in February 1913. The 36-seat bodywork was by Dodson. *AATC*

Below:
The BET group was also an early source of orders. The Worcester Electric Traction Co was a BET subsidiary running electric trams in that city from 1904, and expanded bus operation with a new fleet which included three Daimler 40hp models, one being this charabanc, FK 425, dating from July 1913. In September and October 1914 it was among those pressed into military service. *TWMC*

Above:
A notable early export was the supply of a CC-type double-decker to the Fifth Avenue Coach Co in New York. The basic design was almost completely that of the similar buses built for service in London and other British cities except for the reversal of the rear staircase and entrance to suit the opposite rule of the road. When Fifth Avenue began producing its own buses in 1915 the radiator style was of similar outline. *TWMC*

Left:
The CC was rated as a 3-ton model and some were used as goods vehicles. This tower wagon is thought to have been operated by Bradford Corporation Tramways. *MBRT*

The CD tended to be used as a single-decker. This charabanc was built in 1914 for the Barrow branch of the BET organisation, moving to Sheerness before being acquired by Potteries Electric Traction Co Ltd in 1916. *IAL*

Right:
The CB 2-ton model was of a lighter build. This early example for use by the Daimler works fire brigade is seen outside the fire station — one of the few parts of the Radford works still surviving. *MBRT*

The new model was offered to the British Electric Traction Co Ltd (BET), which had tramways in many parts of Britain and which in January 1912 set up Tramways (MET) Omnibus Co Ltd to run motorbuses in conjunction with its Metropolitan Electric Tramways subsidiary in north London. In that same month, the LGOC was taken over by the Underground group running the main London tube and surface electric rail network of which Albert Stanley, later to become Lord Ashfield, was Managing Director, creating a unified organisation which was to be responsible for the major part of public transport in London. The Associated Equipment Co Ltd was created as a separate Underground subsidiary in June 1912 to take over the LGOC's chassis-building works in Walthamstow, then producing the B-type, with a view to wider sales of its products.

Searle obtained an initial order from BET for the first 100 Daimler buses, including a maintenance contract. He then approached Stanley with that information and the latter proposed placing an order for 250 buses if Daimler would undertake not to supply any other London operator for five years. Searle went back to BET which in due course increased its order to 350, although these tactics alienated both parties. Meanwhile, in May 1912, another BET subsidiary created to operate buses, British Automobile Traction Co Ltd, ordered an initial 10 Daimler buses (later increased to 33), and these began entering service in London in

October that year. Yet before the first of the MET Daimler fleet entered service in January 1913, and thanks to Stanley's negotiating skills (which would influence later Daimler bus history on more than one occasion), an agreement had been reached between the Underground and BET.

The number of Daimler CC buses to be delivered to MET was reduced — 226 were supplied, the balance of 124 being made up by standard B-type chassis — and, to compensate the Daimler Co, in December 1912 it was agreed in principle that Daimler be made sole agent for any vehicles built by AEC and surplus to the requirements of the LGOC or its associated concerns. How this would work was not clarified until December 1913, but it opened the door to large-scale co-operation between the two firms. The plan then agreed was for AEC to build a range of 3-, 4- and 5-ton chassis at Walthamstow for Daimler, which would supply the engines; they were to be badged as and sold by Daimler. An early indication of the line to be followed was provided by the display of a B-type chassis (B2678) with the Daimler 40hp (110 x 150) engine at the Commercial Vehicle Show at Olympia in July 1913. Prototypes of the 3-, 4- and 5-ton types, also with this engine, had been built by January 1914, being given numbers B3010, B2985 and B2960 which were to begin the respective batches ordered; these models became known as Daimler B-types, being derived from the existing B, though with heavier-duty construction.

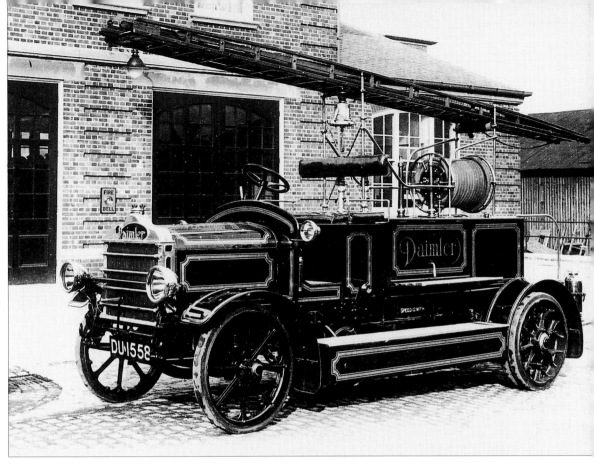

At Coventry, production of the CC and the closely-related CD was to be phased out (although deliveries continued into 1914), and a new 2-ton model, the CB, would take their place. This latter could be described as a scaled-down CC, with 95mm x 140mm 3.97-litre engine known as the '22hp'. As usual at that stage, all these models were used as the basis for either goods or passenger bodywork.

Meanwhile, general sales, notably of the CC, at first often having Dodson double-deck bodywork, and CD, more often a single-decker, were brisk during the brief 1913-14 period when they were on offer. The BET group was a major customer for its provincial as well as London fleets, some run by British Automobile Traction at its various branches and others supplied to subsidiaries; for example, the newly-formed Northern General Transport Co Ltd had 18 CC double-deckers and 11 CD single-deckers in service by early 1914. An unusual venture was that in Oxford, where W. R. Morris, founder of the Morris car business and later to become Lord Nuffield, began a service with seven Daimler CC double-deckers in December 1913, to which the City of Oxford Electric Tramways Co responded with similar vehicles; both these and those of Morris were registered in Coventry, and it seems possible they were readily available as a result of the cancelled MET order. The Tramways Co took over the Morris fleet in 1914.

Daimler also established itself as a supplier of buses to municipal undertakings, a line of business that was to become its forte in later years. Birmingham Corporation, which would ultimately have the largest fleet of Daimler buses, began bus operation with 10 CC double-deckers in July 1913. In 1913-14 Manchester Corporation took eight CC, and Sheffield began bus operation with 15 Daimler buses, seven of the latter being single-deckers.

Daimler ordered batches of the Daimler B from AEC, and numbers of the 3-ton version began to reach operators in 1914, an example being B3025 for United Automobile Services, completed with double-deck body by July. However, the declaration of war with Germany in August stopped further civilian deliveries — within a week, all completed vehicles on Daimler's premises had been commandeered by the War Office. Many buses and lorries already in service were also requisitioned for military use, and ironically the CC buses, possibly the most refined in the country, seem to have been a particular target; the chassis of the MET fleet were returned to Daimler at the rate of 10 per week, fitted with lorry bodies and supplied to the War Office.

New production at both Coventry and Walthamstow was almost completely diverted for military use, at first based on types already in production but then gradually evolving into versions meeting War Office specifications. The 3-ton Daimler B became the W-type, with heavier-duty springs and wheels, followed by an X version with uprated rear hubs, and by March 1915 the first Y-type had

Above:
A CB seen at work, evidently making a delivery of glassware to a Coventry shop, with body slightly tipped to aid unloading. The influence of the War Department on the types it approved was quite strong, with emphasis on reliability and practicality. *MBRT*

Below:
The CB was in production for the Army from soon after the outbreak of war in August 1914, and even those built for civilian use tended to take on a rather military look with features such as the towing hooks and crash-bar in front of the radiator. This example was in use as a coal lorry. *MBRT*

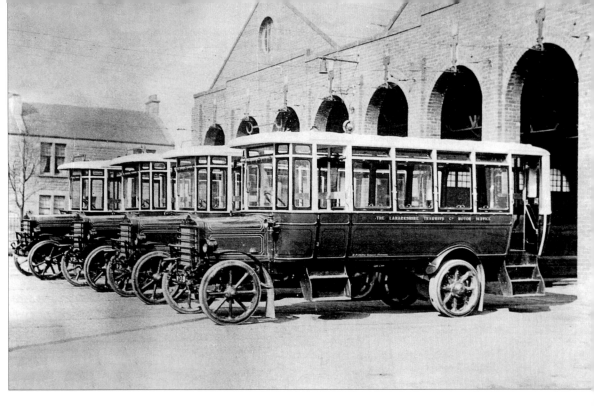

Although wartime production of the 3-ton models, concentrated at AEC's works at Walthamstow, was mainly for military purposes, in 1916 small numbers of the Daimler Y-type by then in production were released to civilian users. This batch was supplied to the Lanarkshire Tramways Co and had bodywork of a fully-enclosed style with well-rounded panels each side of the dash, which was also quite widely favoured for ex-military AEC and Daimler Y-type buses in various company fleets after the war. In 1929, Lanarkshire was to replace its trams with a fleet of Daimler CF6 buses, becoming the Lanarkshire Traction Co, later merged with Central SMT. *MBRT*

appeared, initially as a further minor development, lower-geared and with modified clutch stop. This was destined to be the main wartime product built at Walthamstow, where the factory was extended to allow production to be stepped up. A few were released for use as buses in 1916.

The system of building vehicles at Walthamstow using the Daimler engine and with the Daimler name on the radiator continued until mid-1916; by then AEC had supplied Daimler with 2,761 chassis since the arrangement came into force in 1913, the majority being Y-type military lorries. At Coventry a new factory at Radford, ¼ mile from the existing works, was growing in size; here, the lighter CB22 goods model, again mainly for War Office use, became a major product, although the war effort had immense variety, from staff cars and ambulances to 105hp six-cylinder sleeve-valve engines for heavy-duty track-laying tractors built in conjunction with Foster's of Lincoln. These engines were also chosen for use in the earliest tanks, which went into action for the first time in 1916. There were also aero engines of others' designs as well as complete aircraft. Frank Searle served with distinction in the Tank Corps, his postwar career turning to aviation — he became the first Managing Director of Imperial Airways in 1926.

As the magnitude of the war effort grew, the Government took direct control of war factories from 30 June 1916, and at Walthamstow this meant that chassis were purchased directly from AEC by the War Department, Daimler no longer being involved. From January 1917 AEC began to use engines made by Tylor, such vehicles having radiators bearing AEC lettering, though still of the same outline. There was a period of overlap, output of

Daimler-engined Y-types ceasing in April 1917; however, that of AEC Y-types (designated YA, YB etc) increased, and in December, by mutual consent, the agreement between Daimler and AEC ended upon the expiry of its five-year term. When the war ended in 1918, it was said that Daimler lorry output had totalled about 4,000, and it seems that this was split roughly equally between Walthamstow and Coventry products.

Daimler production of commercial vehicles went through another low-key spell in the period from 1919 to 1925. There were nominally new models, the CJ and CK, from 1919, but these retained the '22hp' four-cylinder sleeve-valve engine of 95mm bore and 140mm stroke, differed in wheelbase lengths of 11ft 6in and 13ft 6in respectively and, all too obviously, were slightly modernised versions of the CB. Birmingham had eight CK2 24-seat buses in 1923, delivered on solid tyres but soon converted to pneumatics, this model being light enough to be among the earliest bus types that could be so fitted. Sales were limited, although this was partly because ex-military chassis could be obtained very cheaply — many bus companies expanded their activities on the strength of fleets of Daimler Y or CB models suitably rebodied.

Two slightly larger models, the CL and CM with 15ft 6in and 16ft wheelbase respectively, appeared in 1925, these having 5.1-litre engines of 104.5mm bore and 150mm stroke, still of four-cylinder form. The basic appearance was barely altered, a minor distinguishing point being smaller Daimler lettering on the radiator, though pneumatic tyres were now usual. At Oxford, the former Tramways company, by now City of Oxford Motor Services Ltd, had continued to favour Daimler buses, having 14 CM-types by 1926, and Manchester received 10 CL in 1925-6, but sales remained low.

It may have been Daimler's awareness that its chassis had become outdated that revived the idea of co-operation with AEC, where forward-control half-cab layout was by then the norm for the larger passenger and goods models. This time the agreement took the form of a joint company, the Associated Daimler Co Ltd, set up on 25 June 1926, with Lord Ashfield (the former Albert Stanley) as Chairman, Daimler being represented on the board by Sir Edward Manville, Percy Martin and R. A. Rotherham. A further key figure was Laurence Pomeroy, already respected as a result of designing the sporting Prince Henry car for Vauxhall in 1912, and who was coming to the end

of a spell designing an 'all-aluminium' car for the Aluminium Company of America. Percy Martin heard of his availability and was able to offer him the post of Chief Engineer of ADC, taken up in October 1926, though his brief was to include consultancy for Daimler and he seems to have operated from Coventry.

The basic idea behind ADC was that AEC, in the process of moving to a new factory at Southall on the western outskirts of London, would build the chassis but that from 1927 most of the engines were to come from Daimler; AEC's relationship with the LGOC as a fellow member of the Underground group was not directly affected. In 1925 Daimler's cars had benefited from the introduction of new six-cylinder sleeve-valve engines, of which the 25/85, of 3.568-litre capacity (81.5mm bore x 114mm stroke), was selected for the planned mainstream ADC applications, becoming the CV25. Meanwhile, existing four-cylinder models of AEC design continued, now badged as ADC. (Fuller details of these are given in the companion *AEC* volume.)

As it turned out, the CV25 engine proved to be far from the step forward claimed — bus work revealed serious shortcomings in its lubrication system. A new single-decker, the 416, with the lower-level frame by then in favour, was offered for 1927 with a choice of the existing four-cylinder, AEC-designed side-valve 5.1-litre engine, known as the 4-type, of conventional (indeed rather dated) design as the 416A, or with the new CV25 as the 416D. After repeated failures, several operators with 416D models converted them to 416A, which proved to be the more popular version. Contrary to earlier intentions, the AEC 4-type engine, slightly updated, was retained in production

Above:
The CM model introduced in 1925 still retained much of the look as set by the CB in 1914, although the Daimler lettering on the radiator was replaced by a small badge. This example was one of four supplied to City of Oxford Motor Services Ltd in 1927, by which date the model had been superseded by the new Associated Daimler range. Hall Lewis built the 26-seat bodywork, of the later charabanc form with glass side windows and centre gangway. *AATC*

Below:
Birmingham Corporation, which had taken 10 Daimler double-deckers as its first buses in 1913 and followed them with 12 on Y-type chassis in 1916, added nine CK2 single-deckers in 1923, this being the first of eight with Strachan & Brown 24-seat bodywork. When new they had solid tyres, as shown, but were quite soon converted to pneumatics, using disc wheels and smaller-section tyres than the 1920 charabanc, with twin tyres on the rear axle. By that time, Birmingham was beginning to build up a large fleet of AEC double-deckers. *MBRT*

— this was already used in the LGOC's standard double-decker of the time, the NS.

There was strong interest in six-wheeled buses at this time, and a new ADC model was the 802, designated 'LS' by the LGOC. The first, LS1, with 68-seat double-deck body, entered service in June 1927, fitted with a Daimler CV35 engine. This was another sleeve-valve 'six', being derived from the 35/120 car engine, of 97mm bore and 130mm stroke and 5.76-litre capacity — a limousine thus powered had been supplied to King George V in 1926. The CV35 had already been chosen by Guy as an option for its new six-wheeled buses in the latter part of 1926; Birmingham Corporation had received one, of type BKX, the 'K' signifying the Knight-type engine. For the 802, there was again a choice of engines, AEC having developed a 7.6-litre six-cylinder engine — in effect a six-cylinder version of the 4-type, though Pomeroy was not in favour of its adoption. In the event, all but four of the 802-model buses had the CV35, but only 20 were built, including a dozen for the LGOC, despite several having been supplied to major operators on a demonstration basis.

Meanwhile, Pomeroy had been busy on a new single-deck design for the November 1927 Commercial Motor Show, offered in forward-control form as model 423 or

Below:
Under the Associated Daimler regime, the basic plan was for chassis bearing the new name to be built by AEC but for Daimler to supply six-cylinder sleeve-valve engines. This example of an ADC 416 with Northern Counties body was posed at the imposing art deco entrance to AEC's new Southall works, which also housed the ADC offices. In practice, as in this case, many 416 models had AEC four-cylinder side-valve engines. *AATC*

bonneted as model 424. There was some resemblance to the 416 in the general layout and frame contours, but these were Coventry-designed models, offered with alternative wheelbase lengths of 16ft 3¼in or 17ft 3⅞in — odd fractions were to be very characteristic of Daimler. They had the CV25 engine, now claimed to be much improved in the latest Mark IV form, and Pomeroy's interest in aluminium alloy led to the use of this material for items such as the gearbox casing, various chassis details and even the wheels. A more modern appearance was given by a new style of radiator, of the same outline as on Daimler cars of the time but without the characteristic fluted top. They were attractive-looking, but troubles persisted and it was decided to put the model into limited production at Coventry, rather than Southall as had been intended, until these were resolved. Consequently, only 73 of the 423 model were built, the largest user being United with 25, though there were 12 for Manchester, 10 for Wrexham & District and eight for Edinburgh. There were 56 of the 424, of which 26 were elegant coaches for Elliott Bros of Bournemouth. The same style of bonnet was applied to AEC-designed chassis, producing types 426 and 427, outwardly very similar yet still using the four-cylinder side-valve AEC 4-type engine, but this simply underlined the failure of the ADC project to gel.

During 1928, the strains in the AEC-Daimler relationship gradually became more and more evident, and on 27 June a divorce was agreed, the two firms going their separate ways. Yet this seems not to have been acrimonious, and indeed an agreement of that date laid down that information on patents should be exchanged with a view to possible licensing arrangements.

Above:
The most ambitious ADC project was the 802 six-wheeled double-decker. Most of the 20 examples built had Daimler 5.76-litre six-cylinder engines, including chassis 802010, built as a demonstrator for Sheffield Corporation and registered WE 2205. It is seen here at Southall in 1928 after bodying by Short Bros. After visiting other operators it was burnt out — the 802 proved to be an ill-fated model. *AATC*

Below:
The ADC 423 and 424 models were designed at Coventry and showed close affinity with Daimler cars of the period, especially in the radiator design, even though it did not incorporate the characteristic fluted top. Seen here at Wells in July 1928, the month after it entered service, is one of 26 coaches built on 424 chassis for the Royal Blue fleet of Elliott Bros of Bournemouth. This one, on chassis 424035, had bodywork by Duple.
G. H. F. Atkins

3. 'Independence' and an Inspired Idea

In the wake of the break-up of Associated Daimler, Laurence Pomeroy was appointed General Manager of the Daimler Co Ltd in September 1928, becoming Managing Director in August 1929. Percy Martin had become Managing Director of the parent BSA company, though still much involved with Daimler. Falling car sales due to the depression had taken Daimler into deficit, and it was important to rebuild Daimler's presence in the bus business.

Pomeroy's immediate response was to upgrade the design of the Daimler-built ADC 423 and 424 models by fitting the CV35 5.76-litre six-cylinder engine (at first quoted as giving 100bhp but then more realistically 85bhp at 2,400rpm) in place of the CV25, thereby creating a new model, the CF6; some, at least, of the initial run of 30 CF6 were converted from stock ADC chassis of both types. The larger-capacity engine fitted quite readily, suggesting this possibility had been foreseen, and indeed some 423 and 424 models already in use were also subsequently fitted with the CV35. The CF6 radiator had the fluted top, looking very like those on contemporary Daimler cars, but otherwise the appearance was almost unaltered.

The CF6 was built in both forward-control and bonneted versions which had the same choice of wheelbase lengths as their predecessors, this now signified by a suffix

Above:
For the CF6, Daimler's first new bus model after the splitting-up of ADC, the only styling change was the adoption of the fluted radiator top, the bonneted version of the model otherwise retaining the outward appearance of the ADC 424, although under that bonnet there was now a larger engine. This example was used as a demonstrator. *TWMC*

S or L to the chassis number, issued in a new series beginning at 7000. In general, even numbers were issued for forward-control chassis and odd numbers for bonneted, though the latter continued only as far as 7323 and it seems that some chassis were rebuilt to forward-control before sale; the even numbers ran to 7998 but with various gaps. Chassis number 7000S was supplied to Whatmough, Gourock, registered HS 5247, this operator also having 7002S and 7004S, while 7001L, 7003L and 7005L were coaches UP 1888/9/7 in the fleet of Glenton Friars of Blaydon.

In the publicity for the CF6, much was made of the attention given to engine lubrication, particularly in minimising oil consumption, which had been difficult to achieve with the Knight sleeve-valve design. This was still a problem, yet, overall, it proved quite a successful model, with an official total of 531 built (of which 126 were evidently laid down as normal-control), mainly between late 1928 and early 1931, though a few remained unsold until 1932.

The larger engine gave sufficient performance and refinement to make the model quite popular as a coach, being chosen by several of the independent operators with services running up the Great North Road to Newcastle; there were also 22 for Elliott Bros' Royal Blue fleet in 1929-30. In 1930 and 1931, some CF6 coaches and at least one horsebox were added to the fleet of the Daimler Hire Co, a subsidiary whose main business was the hire of limousines, which in 1930 became partly owned by Thomas Tilling Ltd and was taken over completely in 1947. Prominent among users of the CF6 in forward-control single-deck bus form were the Lanarkshire Traction Co with 87 and Edinburgh Corporation with 51. The bonneted version was favoured mainly by coach operators, notably Shamrock & Rambler of Bournemouth which had 15, though Lancaster Corporation had a batch with bus bodies.

A double-deck version of the short CF6 chassis was offered, although the narrow front track and small radiator gave such buses rather a top-heavy look. After an initial demonstrator was built in December 1929, 26 more (including three more demonstrators) were completed in 1930, the largest user being Newcastle Corporation with 16, three going to Wallasey Corporation, one each to London independents Redline and Eagle and two, with open-top bodies, to Isle of Thanet. The writer occasionally travelled in some of Newcastle's examples, recalling quite a pronounced low-frequency judder from the clutch on starting from rest, acceleration being fairly modest with typical mellow gearbox sounds of that era. Once speed had built up, they got along quite smoothly, and were well suited to a limited-stop service which was among their regular duties.

It may partly have been realisation of the inadequacies of the CF6 as a double-decker that led to the development of a new chassis design. There was certainly awareness of what the erstwhile ADC partners were doing. G. J. Rackham, appointed Chief Engineer at AEC on the break-up of ADC, had introduced a new double-deck chassis, the

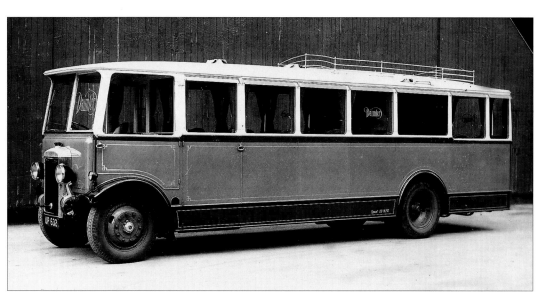

Above:
The close relationship of the CF6 with the ADC 423 and 424 was indicated by this coach (chassis 423005), which was built as an ADC 423 with the plain-topped radiator, fitted with the Short Bros coach body shown and displayed at the 1927 Commercial Motor Show. Early in 1928 it was registered UP 632 and placed in service by J. Glenton Friars of Blaydon on his Great North Road Coach Service between Newcastle and London. It seated only 20 and provided a 'restaurant car' service, with cooked meals collected en route but kept hot in a galley. The vehicle was subsequently returned to Daimler, possibly in a part-exchange deal for new CF6 coaches, and evidently used as a demonstrator, as shown. The CF6 radiator is likely to have been linked to a change to the 5.76-litre engine, as applied to other 423 models in later years. *TWMC*

Below:
The CF6 could look well in half-cab forward-control form, especially if fitted with bodywork of well-proportioned style. This example, with body recorded as being by Abbott of Leicester, was one of a pair used by Charing Cross Hospital in London to carry nurses to and from their accommodation. They were acquired in June 1932 and the Middlesex registrations MV 2591/2 were appropriate to that date, but the chassis numbers 7178S (which had a Grose body) and 7474S suggest construction in 1929 and 1930. It seems likely that they began life as unregistered demonstrators or stock vehicles. *TWMC*

Regent, put into production in the autumn of 1929 and selling very well, as was his previous equivalent model, the Leyland Titan TD1.

The new Daimler, the CG6, to be put into production in the summer of 1930, although retaining the 5.76-litre sleeve-valve engine and conventional gearbox, paid the Regent the compliment of having similarly neat front-end design including a deeper, slimmer version of the Daimler radiator and a frame of almost identical design. It also virtually matched its 15ft 6½in wheelbase — that of the CG6 double-deck model was just ⅛in longer, and of the single-decker was identical to the equivalent new AEC Regal at 17ft. There was thus strong evidence of continuing design contact with AEC. New chassis number series began at 8000 for single-deck models and 9000 for double-deckers and the basis had been created for Daimler's bus range as built through the next decade. All were to be of forward-control layout.

The CG6 was to prove a very rare model — Stockton Corporation was to be the largest single user with four double-deckers, chassis number 9008 with Park Royal body in 1930, followed by 9013, 9022 and 9026 bodied by Brush in 1931. The initial double-deck chassis, number 9000, was sold off, becoming a van with an Edinburgh furniture remover; 9017 also became a van and another double-deck chassis, 9012, eventually became a single-deck coach for Greatrex of Stafford. What is thought to have been the only CG6 single-deck model sold as such, 8013, was supplied to Edinburgh Corporation in 1931. It seems that about 30 CG6 had been laid down, much as with the CF6, but two significant developments were to cause most to be rebuilt to the succeeding CH6 or CP6 specifications before sale.

The first development was the introduction of what Daimler christened its fluid flywheel transmission. The initial basis was the fluid coupling invented by Professor H. Fottinger for the Vulcan shipyard in Hamburg in 1905, but adapted for vehicle use by Harold Sinclair, becoming known as the Vulcan-Sinclair coupling. The basic idea was that oil in a doughnut-shaped internally-vaned casing replacing the engine flywheel was impelled by centrifugal force and channelled towards the vanes in a similarly-shaped driven member housed within the same casing but not mechanically connected to it. As engine speed increased the driven member would also begin to rotate, accelerating with perfect smoothness until, at higher speeds, the two rotated at almost the same rate.

The fluid flywheel transmission had obvious benefits for a vehicle making repeated restarts, and in October 1926 Sinclair initiated discussions with the London General Omnibus Co Ltd. Trials were subsequently made on an ADC bus chassis, thought to have been a 416. It may have been the break-up of ADC that delayed further progress in regard to buses, and there was the drawback when used with a conventional sliding-mesh gearbox that a clutch was still needed to free the drive completely to allow gear changes to be made. However, Percy Martin was keen to apply the idea to cars; a 30hp Double Six model is known to have been running experimentally with this system in March 1929, and was briefly offered for sale from May 1930.

An at least equally important (but hitherto separate) line of development was the preselective epicyclic gearbox invented by Walter Gordon Wilson, derived from earlier work going back to 1901 and including wartime tank transmission systems. Sets of small gear wheels, revolving within internally-toothed annulus wheels and coupled together, were arranged to give the desired gear ratio when the appropriate annulus was held stationary by its external brake band. Gear changes were made by pressing and releasing a pedal replacing the normal clutch pedal, the next ratio required being selected in advance by a small

Left:
By July 1929, Glenton Friars of Blaydon had moved on to this style of 26-seat coach body, built by Hoyal at Weybridge. Two vehicles were placed in service, based on long-wheelbase CF6 chassis 7190L and 7192L, registered UP 3232/3. These and four other CF6 coaches dating from 1930 were taken over, along with the London service, by United Automobile Services Ltd in March 1932. Further CF6 coaches were also acquired from other sources to add to United's own, and by 1935 the resulting D class numbered 43 vehicles, most of the coaches being rebodied as buses. *TWMC*

Above:
Viewed about 70 years on, a bonneted CF6 with the style of coach body associated with the type looks supremely elegant. At the time, its appeal was largely that of looking and sounding like an enlarged Daimler limousine — the 35hp car using the same basic engine was still in production — yet within a few years it would have been regarded as simply out of date. This 1930 example, NH 9866, on chassis 7247S with Duple 24-seat body, was one of a dozen bonneted CF6 models used by Allchin & Son of Northampton on a network of express routes acquired by the United Counties Omnibus Co Ltd in November 1933. *TWMC*

Left:
Newcastle Corporation was the largest user of the CF6 double-decker, with a fleet of 16 with 54-seat Brush bodywork dating from July-August 1930. Seen here near Eldon Square is No 112 (VK 2387) on chassis 7436S. Like most of the batch, it was withdrawn in 1938.
R. C. Davis collection

Above:
The styles of bodywork supplied to London independent operators, influenced by the conservative ideas of the Public Carriage Office of the Metropolitan Police, often contrasted with those favoured elsewhere. This CF6, chassis 7398S with 56-seat body by Birch Bros, dated from 1930; registered GC 7388, it was operated by the Eagle Omnibus Co Ltd and is seen in East Ham on service 15 to Ladbroke Grove. When taken over by London Transport in November 1933, it was numbered DST4, but ran only briefly as such, being sold and scrapped in 1935.
The Omnibus Society

Below:
J. Bullock & Sons Ltd, of Featherstone, which used the fleetname 'B & S', took delivery of two CF6 coaches with bodywork by Taylor of Barnsley in March 1930. No 113 (HL 4743) on chassis 7382S is seen here at Scarborough three months later. *G. H. F. Atkins*

Above:
The CG6 marked the beginning of a complete new generation of models, yet proved very rare in itself. This one, chassis number 9008, is thought to have been the first to join an operator's fleet, becoming Stockton Corporation 57 (UP 4743) during 1930; the registration batch also included a Leyland Titan TD1, a Lion LT2 and an AEC Regal 4, although the CG6 is not recorded as having been sold by Daimler until July 1932. The 52-seat body, by Park Royal, was to a style also built on contemporary AEC Regent chassis. *TWMC*

Left:
The new 'face', with deeper, restyled radiator, as standard for the CG6 and adopted for the CH6 later in 1930, put Daimler into the forefront of bus styling trends. AEC had introduced a tidier front end with an elegant radiator for the Regent in 1929, but Daimler made a virtue of necessity by extending the casing downwards to include an oil cooler required with the sleeve-valve engine. *IAL*

Above:
This unregistered CH6 demonstrator was used for the *Modern Transport* road test of the new fluid flywheel transmission in October 1930 and may have been the first to have been bodied. Park Royal, then somewhat in favour for Daimler double-deck demonstrators, built the lowbridge body, incorporating minor styling changes adopted for much of that firm's 1931 output. *IAL*

lever on the steering column. The Wilson gearbox had been put into production by Armstrong Siddeley on its 20hp and 30hp cars in time for the 1929 Motor Show, and a company set up jointly by John Siddeley and Walter Wilson to share royalties from the invention.

Following talks between Wilson, Martin and Pomeroy, Siddeley's own 30hp Armstrong Siddeley car with Wilson gearbox was fitted with a fluid flywheel at the Daimler works at Easter 1930. The combination proved almost ideal, as the fluid flywheel eliminated the severe judder on starting from rest which had proved a drawback of the Wilson 'box used on its own, relying as it did on the inherently fierce action of brake bands to obtain the various ratios — an experimental Wilson 'box installation made in 1929 in an LGOC NS double-decker had been abandoned

because of the rough take-off. With the fluid flywheel, the driver, having preselected first or second gear, pressed and fully released the gear-change pedal to engage the desired ratio before pressing the accelerator, whereupon the fluid flywheel ensured a smooth start from rest.

Daimler was granted licences to make Wilson gearboxes, though meanwhile buying them from Armstrong Siddeley. The Daimler Co and Martin patented the combination of the fluid flywheel and Wilson gearbox, which was offered on Daimler cars from July 1930 but denied to car makers outside the BSA group, this applying even to Armstrong Siddeley following a brief period when fluid flywheels were supplied to that firm.

The CH6 bus model was, in effect, the CG6 with fluid flywheel and four-speed Wilson gearbox. Early gearboxes for this model were supplied by Armstrong Siddeley, until Daimler's own manufacture got underway. The standard preselector control was a lever working in a quadrant on the steering column, this becoming characteristic of Daimler buses for over 20 years. Such was the confidence in the new transmission's merits that the CG6 was dropped almost immediately; no conventional gearbox option was offered until 1958. The early examples appear to have been

Above:
Of immense importance in the history of British bus development were the three Daimler CH6 buses placed in service by the LGOC from Harrow Weald garage in January 1931. They had been fitted with virtually standard ST-type LGOC bodies and DST2 (GK 5415) with chassis 9025 is seen here when almost new. Ironically, the drivers thus given the benefit of the future standard

London bus transmission system had to do without a windscreen until officialdom conceded the need for this 'luxury' later in the year. The buses were withdrawn in 1935, the bodies being transferred to new AEC Regent chassis specially built in 1936 to the obsolete ST class length, but DST2's chassis was to live on as a single-decker with Ernie Hartness of Penrith until 1950. *The Omnibus Society*

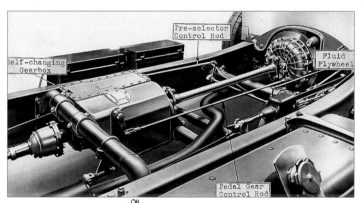

Left:
This view of the transmission layout in one of the first CH6 chassis was published in *Modern Transport* of 1 November 1930. Amidships-mounting of conventional gearboxes was starting to go out of favour, but the depth of the 'self-changing' epicyclic gearbox above its centre-line forced the retention of this position for reasons related to the floor level and ground clearance rules; as it turned out, this proved beneficial in helping to cool both fluid flywheel and gearbox. The gearbox shown would almost certainly have been of Armstrong Siddeley manufacture. *IAL*

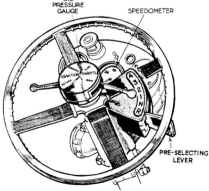

Left:
The quadrant type of preselector lever just under the steering wheel was to be characteristic of Daimler buses for over 20 years. In theory, it was logical, the driver usually moving the lever up (or down) one notch at a time before making the desired change by pressing and releasing the gear-change pedal. In practice it was not always easy to judge just which ratio had been last preselected, especially in the dark. This sketch shows one on an early CH6, having smaller ignition, advance and retard and hand-throttle levers above the steering wheel boss. *AATC*

Above:
An early example of the CH6 in single-deck form was GP 689 (chassis 8008), supplied in May 1931 to C. E. Holmes, trading as West London Coaches, of London W9, which ran a London-Aylesbury coach service. The body has been quoted as Duple, but this photograph reveals several Harrington characteristics, suggesting that the body which it is reported as carrying in later years may have been the original seen here. It became London Transport DST6 on takeover of the business in January 1934, this vehicle being sold in 1938. *TWMC*

Right:
The CP6, with a new poppet-valve engine, was announced in October 1931. This example (chassis 9073) is thought to have been the first built as such, being displayed with Park Royal 52-seat body at that year's Show. It was in Newcastle Corporation livery, becoming No 152 in that fleet, registered VK 7134, in June 1932. It is seen here near Sough Top in Derbyshire, while being road-tested for *Modern Transport. IAL*

Right:
The general appearance of the sleeve-valve engine as fitted to CH6 models is conveyed by this illustration of an Edinburgh Corporation single-decker, published in *Modern Transport* in November 1932, although this particular engine had been modified to allow the use of creosote as an alternative fuel, with additional equipment visible just behind the headlamp. *IAL*

drawn from the stock of CG6 chassis, numbered from 9000 to about 9030, converted to or completed as CH6, though some of these still in stock in 1932 were renumbered, evidently to disguise their early origin. By October, a Park Royal-bodied demonstrator was being used for press road tests — this may have been 9019, registered VC 6779, although 9011, also bodied by Park Royal, was registered in Glasgow as GG 1393 for demonstration to the Corporation there in November; both were later sold to Dundee Corporation.

The most influential early CH6 models were chassis 9023-5, delivered to the London General Omnibus Co in December 1930 where they received bodies to the style then being fitted to ST class AEC Regent buses, entering service in January 1931 as DST1, 3 and 2 respectively. The transmission greatly impressed, even if the sleeve-valve engine did not, and Lord Ashfield used his legendary negotiating skills to persuade Daimler to grant AEC a licence to allow use of the fluid transmission system, under the provision for continued co-operation agreed at the break-up of ADC in 1928. This not only covered the supply of Daimler-built units for LGOC buses, but also allowed the system to be offered on AEC models for general sale, a privilege not granted to any other competitor. Over 300 sets were supplied (including 174 in London LT or STL buses and 24 special gearboxes to suit the reverse rotation of the

side-engined Q model) before AEC began making its own such units under licence early in 1934, by which time the total sold in Daimler's own buses was only about 255.

Although the CH6 aroused widespread interest, sales remained modest. Many operators put demonstrators into service and some purchased single vehicles to assess its merits, a noteworthy example of the latter being Crosville (normally a Leyland user), which received single-deck chassis number 8000 in May 1931. Manchester and Sheffield Corporations each purchased one double-decker, but neither placed a repeat order. However, municipalities in northeast England were becoming a Daimler stronghold, largely on the basis of the CH6 — Middlesbrough, Newcastle, Stockton and West Hartlepool placed 16, 10, six and two CH6 double-deckers in service respectively during 1931, and other municipal users included York, Birkenhead and Luton. Edinburgh Corporation received a CH6 single-decker on double-deck type chassis 9031 in November 1930 and nine single-deckers in 1932. The model remained available after the introduction of the CP6 described below; a few more were built in 1932-3, while others were converted to CP6 specification. In all, about 77 double-deckers and 53 single-deckers were sold in CH6 form.

By 1931, Daimler's sleeve-valve engine was well past its sell-by date; directly comparable standards of quietness were attainable from six-cylinder engines with conventional poppet valves, notably those from Leyland and AEC, and these did not have the problem of heavy consumption of lubricating oil. As early as 1927 Pomeroy had suggested the production of a poppet-valve equivalent of the CV35 engine, retaining as much of the original as possible, and he did just that for the new CP6 model announced in October 1931. The stroke was unchanged at 130mm but elimination of the double sleeves allowed the bore to go up to 103.5mm and hence the swept volume became 6.561 litres. Overhead valves operated by push-rods were adopted and the quoted power was 90bhp at 2,400rpm, rather less than the latest AEC and Leyland petrol engines but giving adequate performance, aided by the transmission.

What may have been the first CP6 (having the lowest known engine number associated with the type although possibly built as a CH6) was a single-decker demonstrator on chassis number 8010, registered VC 9799 in October 1931; this was later acquired by Lanarkshire Traction Co, which from March 1932 placed 20 new CP6 with Pickering bodies in service, two CH6 coaches being added in 1933. Among CP6 double-deckers, the first built as such seems likely to have been 9073, with Park Royal body, for the Commercial Motor Show in November 1931 and used as a demonstrator in Newcastle livery before being added

to that fleet, registered as VK 7134, in June 1932. There were several early instances of conversions from CH6 to CP6, notably a single-decker, 8004, supplied to West Yorkshire Road Car Co Ltd in March 1931 and evidently converted later in the year, and double-deck chassis 9006, a demonstrator registered in Leeds in January 1931 as UB 4953 (too early to have been a CP6 from new, unless used as a prototype) but later sold to Cardiff.

The CP6 proved to be Daimler's final petrol-engined bus model, the majority being delivered to operators in 1932-4. A revised wheelbase length of 16ft 3³⁄₁₆in (still only fractionally different from AEC's 16ft 3in) was introduced for the double-deck version during 1932. Gradually the list of customers grew, the overwhelming majority of double-deckers being built for municipalities. Hull had 20, and important landmarks were orders from Coventry for 19 and Birmingham for 10. Hitherto, Coventry had tended to favour its other native bus builder, Maudslay; Birmingham had been one of AEC's most important provincial customers since the early 1920s, but favoured Morris-Commercial (based in the city) during that firm's brief spell as a builder of full-sized buses, before receiving the 10 CP6 buses in the winter of 1933-4. The latter proved to be the only examples of the type in that fleet, yet they marked the beginning of a 40-year spell during which Daimler supplied

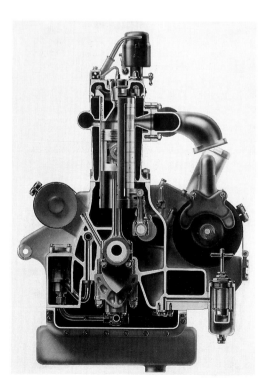

The comparison between CH6 and CP6 engines is conveyed in these two cross-sectional views from October 1931, which also reveal how the latter retained much of the bottom-end design of the former. The CH6 view, *left*, shows how the inner and outer sleeves, in which slots opened the inlet and exhaust ports, were driven by miniature con-rods from the eccentric shaft. In the CP6, *right*, the latter was replaced by a camshaft, with push-rods and rockers to operate the overhead valves. *IAL*

Above:

Many Daimler demonstrators of the early 1930s led complex lives. This one, KV 1396 (chassis 9064), had Brush bodywork and was first registered in July 1932. The picture suggests that it began life as a CH6 or CP6, and it is seen painted for demonstration to Westcliff-on-Sea Motor Services Ltd. However, its most influential duty, following conversion to Gardner 5LW power, was to act as demonstrator of the new COG5 model (described in the next chapter) to Birmingham Corporation, ultimately the biggest user of the type. It was later sold in that form to County Motor Services of Stakeford, Northumberland, and passed to United in 1937. *P. M. Battersby collection*

most of Birmingham's buses. Single-deckers were rarer, though Yorkshire Traction took six CP6 coaches in 1933; six were exported to Spain in 1932 and there were a number of independent operators which chose the type, usually as coaches.

The CP6 remained available until autumn 1937, but few were built after 1935 and the last, in 1936, were a pair for J. Bullock & Sons of Featherstone. The total numbers sold from new as CP6 are estimated as 112 double-deck and 48 single-deck — still modest figures, although the 1932-4 period had been poor for bus sales generally.

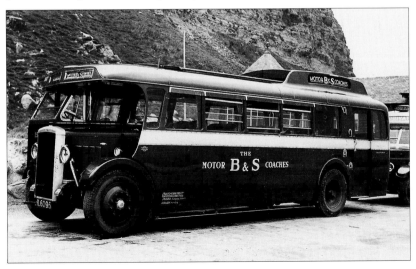

Left:

J. Bullock & Sons continued to purchase Daimlers from time to time for its B & S fleet. This CP6, dating from 1934, had 32-seat coach bodywork by Charles Roberts Ltd. Numbered 158 (HL 6095), it had chassis number 8093 and is seen at Scarborough. B & S was to prove the final customer for the CP6, two single-deck examples being delivered in 1936. *G. H. F. Atkins*

Above:
The Yorkshire Traction Co Ltd, a TBAT subsidiary with headquarters in Barnsley, standardised on Leyland vehicles but placed this CP6 (chassis 9124) in service as its 366, registered HE 5771, in August 1932. The Short Bros lowbridge body, of modern outline for that date, seated 52. A new style of bonnet side, with larger, square-cut louvres towards the front end, had recently been introduced. *TWMC*

Below:
Yorkshire Traction returned with an order for six CP6 single-deckers, delivered in May 1933 for the long-distance service to London, the bodies, built by Brush to British Electrical Federation design, having coach seating for 28 passengers. The vehicle seen here in Nottingham in August 1934 was No 371 (HE 5994) on chassis 8085. They were withdrawn in 1946 after being hired to the War Department from 1940, though the bodies were transferred to 1935 Leyland Tiger TS7 chassis of which the Leyland metal-framed bodies were in poor condition.
G. H. F. Atkins

4. The Gardner Route to Success

Daimler was quite slow off the mark in regard to the adoption of diesel engines (in those days more usually described as oil engines) for its buses, nothing being offered publicly before late 1933, three years after both AEC and Crossley introduced own-make engines, admittedly not without early problems. Pomeroy is thought to have learned something of the development of such engines for road use by Mercedes-Benz early in 1927 when he visited that firm, but it seems likely that Daimler's poor financial position ruled out the type of research needed to produce its own design at that stage.

The course eventually adopted was the purchase of engines from a proprietary manufacturer, L. Gardner & Sons Ltd, of Patricroft, near Manchester. In view of the reputation later built up by that firm's LW series of engines, introduced for road transport work in September 1931, it is surprising in hindsight that a Daimler so fitted did not appear for a further two years, being displayed for the first time at the Commercial Motor Show in November 1933. Yet history proved it to be a sound choice, opening up a far bigger market for Daimler buses than ever before.

Unusually, the Gardner LW was available in a five-cylinder form as well as four- and six-cylinder versions. The bore and stroke were 4¼in and 6in respectively, and this gave the 5LW a swept volume of 7.0 litres, giving an output of 85bhp at the very conservative governed speed of 1,700rpm. Its external dimensions were comparable to those of most six-cylinder bus engines suitable for use in double-deckers and, in regard to Daimler, the power rating matched those of the CH6 or CP6 quite closely. The combination of the Daimler chassis and the 5LW, given the designation COG5, produced a very economical and reliable bus, and the fluid transmission helped mask the modest performance and absorbed some of the harshness

Below:
This scene of activity in Daimler's bus assembly shop at Radford works dates from about August 1934, just as output of Birmingham Corporation's third order in rapid succession for the COG5, for 100 chassis, was getting underway. Happily for historians, it was the practice at Daimler, as elsewhere in those days, to chalk the chassis number on the front dash, and hence it is possible to identify 9275 in the foreground and 9281 in the centre of the picture, which respectively became Birmingham 642 and 684, with matching AOG registration numbers. Most of the other chassis visible were for the same order, but three at the back of the left-hand row are identifiable as the first three of the COA6 model, with AEC 8.8-litre oil engines, for Coventry. This scene would have been much quieter a year or two previously, when bus chassis output had been down to an average of barely two per week before the COG5 — and especially Birmingham's commitment to it — transformed the situation. *AATC*

Above:
A pair of COG5 double-deck demonstrators were registered ADU 470 and 471 in September 1934. Both had Weymann metal-framed bodies, Daimler's usual choice in the mid-1930s, this being the second one, on chassis 9226, which went to Bradford Corporation as its No 394. It was well-liked and taken into stock but considered rather underpowered for that hilly city, and the COG6 was chosen for later deliveries. The other bus of the pair, ADU 470, went to Isle of Thanet Electric Supply Co, which bought four similar COG5 buses. The sloping radiator and full-length row of square-cut bonnet louvres were characteristic of most COG models. *IAL*

Below:
The early COG5 single-deckers had the same sloping radiator as the double-deck version of this model. Among the first was a batch of four with Weymann composite 32-seat bodies for South Shields Corporation, also dating from September 1934, this being No 107 (CU 3205) on chassis 8098. It was reported a few months later that they were giving between 11.79 and 12.55mpg on local services. *AATC*

of that engine. As many municipalities embarked on the replacement of some or all of their tram routes with bus services, the fluid transmission assumed added significance, as drivers of electric trams, especially if middle-aged, often had difficulty in learning how to drive crash-gearbox buses.

There are two candidates for the earliest bus to go out to operators in this form. One was a double-decker, chassis 9064, evidently built as a CH6 or possibly CP6 demonstrator — the chassis number suggests late 1931 construction and the style of the Brush body was in favour that year, but it was first registered in July 1932 as KV 1396. A photograph shows it with that registration and the style of radiator and bonnet as standard up to mid-1932, painted in the livery of Westcliff-on-Sea Motor Services Ltd; it seems almost certain that it was still petrol-engined at that stage. More importantly, KV 1396, by then converted to COG5 specification, spent a month with Birmingham Corporation, reportedly in 1933, which must rank as one of the most fruitful spells of demonstration by any bus as, from 1934 to 1939, the COG5 was to be that city's standard choice. It was sold to a Northumberland independent operator, County Motor Services, of Stakeford near Choppington, and in 1937 passed to United, in which fleet it remained until withdrawal in 1947. (For much of that time, it was seen almost daily by the author, then unaware of its historical importance.) By then it had the sloping radiator characteristic of standard COG5 models; this style may have been inspired by the type of radiator found on

Above:
Coventry Corporation embarked on a policy of favouring Daimler chassis with AEC oil engines with the delivery of the first three COA6 models to be built, in November 1934, this one being No 117 (KV 9117) on chassis 9222. They had A165-type engines of 8.8-litre capacity, a type then still the standard oil engine in AEC's own chassis, where the radiator projected forward 4½in when so fitted. Daimler's installation was neater and, as with later COA6 models, used a vertical radiator. Metro-Cammell built the body to the operator's specification, very similar to contemporary Brush-built buses on CP6 chassis. *IAL*

Maudslay's six-cylinder bus models, some of which were in service in Coventry, though sloping radiators were then coming into fashion on some cars.

A single-deck counterpart was chassis 8072, built as a CH6 in 1932 but converted to COG5, bodied by Willowbrook as a 32-seat bus, registered KV 5822 and used as a demonstrator until sold to Bunty Motorways of Coventry in 1936. At the Commercial Motor Show in November 1933 a COG5 double-deck chassis was on display on Daimler's stand, although this was a 'borrowed' chassis (9132) from Coventry's CP6 order and entered service with petrol engine and Brush body in March 1934 with the rest of the batch. There was also a COG5 single-decker with a Weymann bus body, this being chassis 8091 for Edinburgh Corporation, which would enter service in 1934 — another case of a prestigious customer won over by the type. That undertaking had earlier tried creosote as a fuel, using a CH6.

Above:
Among the first customers for the COG6, with six-cylinder Gardner 6LW engine, was Cape Town Tramways, with an initial dozen with Weymann 56-seat double-deck bodies built in the latter part of 1935, the model being adopted thereafter as the fleet's standard type until wartime. This garage line-up includes three of a batch of four built in 1937 on the same COG6 double-deck model chassis but which received 31-seat single-deck bodies, also by Weymann. Some of the double-deckers, including that nearest the camera (No 95 on chassis 9253), come from the original 1935 batch, others from later deliveries. *AATC*

Above left:
The North East of England was fertile ground for Daimler bus sales, and Sunderland Corporation joined the users with an initial pair of COG5 models with Roe centre-entrance 48-seat bodies; No 27 (GR 1190) on chassis 9247 joined the fleet in November 1934, remaining in service until April 1952. The COG5 with basically similar bodywork was adopted as standard for the fleet until 1939, and Daimler remained the main supplier until 1966. *AATC*

Left:
Newcastle Corporation chose Armstrong-Saurer engines for 10 single-deckers placed in service in May 1935, thereby giving rise to the COS4 type. They had vertical radiators, giving an appearance much like a CP6. Metro-Cammell built the body on No 164 (BTN 104) based on chassis 8119. *AATC*

Alternative engines were also being tried out, and Daimler seems to have tried to retain an open-minded approach. Chassis 8077, built as a CH6, was fitted with a four-cylinder Tangye VM4 oil engine — this concern being one of several proprietary engine manufacturers which made brief attempts to get into a promising market — being redesignated COT4 and then also sold to Edinburgh; it was re-engined again in 1935, becoming a COG5.

More significantly, Coventry Corporation, influenced by the preferences of R. A. Fearnley, General Manager of its transport undertaking, began a period of standardisation on AEC oil engines in Daimler chassis, creating type COA6, although that designation was to include several variants. The first batch was of three fitted with the A165 8.8-litre engine (115mm x 142mm) with Ricardo Comet indirect injection developing up to 130bhp, delivered in November 1934. This engine was then about to be superseded as AEC's standard type for most models by the A171 Comet-head unit of nominal 7.7-litre size (105mm x 146mm, though the true swept volume given by these dimensions was 7.58 litres). In late 1934 an early example of this latter engine was fitted to KV 64, a CP6 demonstrator (chassis 9074 dating from December 1931) which had run for Ashton Corporation but was supplied to Coventry (initially on loan) in 1933.

Another CP6 (chassis 9111), originally built for the 1931 Show and given Northumberland registration JR 1891 when sold to the County fleet in May 1934, received a Leyland oil engine, being then designated COL6; in 1935 Bury

Above:
Hull Corporation standardised on the COG5 in 1936 and 1937, with batches of 20 and 15 double-deckers having Weymann composite bodywork. The undertaking was an early user of a 'streamline' style of livery. This view of No 158 (CAT 159) on chassis 9677 captures the 'look' of the COG5 admirably. *TWMC*

Above right:
The COG5/40 was a new version of the COG5 single-decker in which the front-end layout was made as compact as possible. Wolverhampton Corporation had inherited some rural services formerly run by the Great Western Railway, and some of its single-deckers had roof luggage-carriers which, unusually, were provided with ladder access from the nearside front. This feature is shown by No 315 (JW 8115), on chassis 8184, one of six 34-seat buses with Park Royal body, dating from 1936. Like many COG5 buses of the time, these had five-speed gearboxes. *AATC*

Right:
This scene dating from late 1936 shows two COG5/40 chassis — numbers 8281 and 8282 — being assembled for export to Springs Municipality in the Transvaal, South Africa. Although the COG5/40 was mainly a home-market model, some were exported where operating conditions were considered suitable. Another Gardner 5LW engine is being prepared for fitting to a further chassis and, in the background on the left, two double-deck chassis frames marked 'Edinburgh' are visible, being part of that city's second order for COG6 models. *IAL*

Right:
Birmingham Corporation was by far the biggest user of the
COG5 model. Deliveries soon built up from the initial 30 of early
1934 and reached a peak in 1937, when some 216 entered
service, including No 1023 (CVP 123) seen in August of that
year; the chromium-plated radiator was then a newly-introduced
option. The body was built to Birmingham's rather quirky
standard design by Metro-Cammell, superbly finished in the
distinctive dark blue and cream livery — no external advertise-
ments were carried. The bus is crossing the junction of Hill Street
and Navigation Street in a landscape behind New Street station
long since lost to redevelopment. Note the Midland Red QL-type
bus of 1928 on the left. *G. H. F. Atkins*

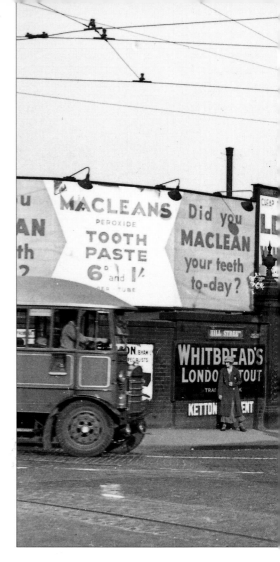

Corporation carried out a similar conversion of five CP6
double-deckers dating from 1932.

Yet another variant was created in August 1934 when
chassis 9168, one of three CP6 double-deckers sold to
Newcastle Corporation the previous October, was fitted
with an Armstrong-Saurer 8.55-litre six-cylinder oil
engine, Daimler records showing it as converted to type
COS6. This was partly a matter of support for local industry, for Armstrong-Saurer Commercial Vehicles Ltd was
based in Scotswood Works, Newcastle. The Saurer company
in Switzerland had just introduced a new engine, known as
the dual turbulence type, with direct injection and intro-
ducing the idea of a toroidal cavity in the piston which
would later be widely adopted by other manufacturers. Ten
single-deckers with a four-cylinder version of this engine,
also for Newcastle and delivered early in 1935, were designated COS4; in 1938 these passed to United together
with a route running beyond the city boundary. By mid-
wartime there were problems keeping them in service,
Armstrong-Saurer having been closed down in 1937. Parts

from Switzerland were then unobtainable, so the buses
were fitted with AEC petrol engines, at first running on
producer gas under the Government scheme.

Despite the work on alternative engines, it was the
COG5 that began to be built in greater quantities from
early 1934. A major factor in this was a series of substantial orders from Birmingham, mostly double-deckers, the
bulk bodied in that city by Metro-Cammell or the Birmingham Railway Carriage & Wagon Co to the operator's
distinctive specification. There were an initial 30, then
60 delivered in 1934-5 and 100 in 1935 plus 35 single-
deckers, and so it went on. Yet it was by no means only
Birmingham that took to the COG5. The municipal fleets
of Aberdare, Sunderland, Stockton, Newcastle and Luton,
as well as Bullock & Sons, all received double-deck examples in 1934 and early 1935. The single-deck version was
supplied to South Shields, Wolverhampton and Aberdare,
as well as the South Wales Transport Co Ltd, in the same
period, and, while none of these orders was large, all of the
municipalities placed repeat orders.

A further extension to the range came towards the end of 1935 with the building of the first batch of COG6 models for Edinburgh Corporation, which was to become the largest British user of the type, with 43 by 1939. These had the Gardner 6LW engine, having the same 4¼in bore and 6in stroke as the 5LW but with six cylinders, the swept volume becoming 8.4 litres and the output 102bhp; the additional engine length was accommodated by extending the bonnet rearwards. With typical double-deck unladen weight figures in that period of around 6¾ tons, this was sufficient to produce a lively bus with good hill-climbing capability, at which the COG5 was no more than mediocre, and the bonus of a more appealing and smoother sound than the rather clattery 5LW. The initial batch of 16 had chassis numbers 9471-86, and were delivered with Metro-Cammell bodies between November 1935 and January 1936. Before these had entered service, 10 COG6 chassis were delivered to Weymann for bodying prior to export for Cape Town Tramways (this concern ultimately having 46 such buses and the associated Port Elizabeth Tramways

fleet a further 39). Single COG6 examples or demonstrators went to Aberdeen, Bradford and the oddly-named Stalybridge, Hyde, Mossley & Dukinfield Joint Transport Board, all of which soon ordered COG6 batches.

There was also further development of the COG5. A five-speed version of the preselective gearbox became available, the additional ratio being a lower first gear, normally used with a higher-geared rear axle to help overcome the restricted speed range of the Gardner engine while taking advantage of its good torque. It was available from 1935, being quite often specified for single-deckers — among early instances were Newcastle's COS4 buses — but a minority of operators specified it for COG5 double-deckers, Sunderland's and some of Newcastle's being examples. Another change was the adoption of vacuum-hydraulic operation of the brakes in place of the triple-servo system used on early vehicles.

By November 1936, flexible engine mounting was adopted as standard for all Gardner-engined Daimler buses. This was quite remarkable in the way it softened the

Right:
The Bombay Electrical
Supply & Tramways Co
began a lengthy spell as a
regular Daimler customer
with 20 COG5 double-
deckers dating from late
1937, the bodywork being
built in the BEST workshops.
A further 50 similar buses
were supplied in 1939.
TWMC

sound level within a COG5 so that engine noise became less prominent than the rather agreeable tones from the Wilson gearbox, even though, outwardly, the staccato bark was still clearly evident.

A new version of the COG5 single-decker had been introduced in late 1935. This was the COG5/40, the suffix intended to indicate the potential seating capacity; in practice, while 39 was quite often achieved, only a couple of buses built in 1936 for Lancaster Corporation, with a rearward-facing row of five seats at the front, seem to have reached 40 within the home-market 27ft 6in length limit then in force. Yet it was quite an achievement to reduce the bonnet length housing a Gardner 5LW engine, not a very compact unit, to 3ft 11½in — about 8in less than the standard COG5; the radiator did not have the sloping front, reverting to a style more like that of the petrol models, and the engine did not have a fan. There was a degree of overlap of types but most later home-market COG5 single-deckers were COG5/40 models. Numerically the first COG5/40 was chassis 8172 for the Potteries concern, which was to become one of two BET-controlled companies to take batches of both this model and COG5 double-deckers in the period up to 1940, the other being

Trent — these two companies built up total COG5 fleets of 60 and 50 respectively — although East Kent also acquired five COG5 double-deckers when it took over the Isle of Thanet concern. Edinburgh Corporation received 20 COG5/40 with Weymann bodies in 1936, building up to a total of 65 similar buses by 1938.

Coventry took new 7.7-litre COA6 double-deckers, beginning with 20 in 1935 and building up to 92 by 1939, these differing from contemporary COG5 or COG6 double-deckers in having vertical radiators; there were other details showing distinct touches of AEC practice. The earlier batches had A171 Ricardo-head indirect-injection engines as built, but some in later batches had the new A173 direct-injection version, adopted as standard from 1939 in much the same way as tended to happen with contemporary AEC buses. The COA6 types did not have flexible engine mountings.

Important changes in Daimler's management occurred in the mid-1930s. Percy Martin retired in October 1935, to be replaced as BSA Group Chairman by Geoffrey D. Burton. The latter had a disagreement over car policy with Laurence Pomeroy, who left the Daimler company in May 1936, F. H. Ayres becoming Managing Director. The

Above:

Daimler sales to independent coach operators became quite rare in the mid- to late 1930s, even though the COG5/40 was a good deal more refined a model from the passengers' viewpoint than was perhaps judged from the rather clattery external sound from the 5LW engine. A small but loyal customer was J. J. Granter, trading as United Services, of Upton, near Pontefract, the example shown, with Duple 35-seat body, being CWT 635 on chassis 8344, which was exhibited at the Commercial Motor Show in November 1937. It was the second such coach of generally similar design; a third body to this style was built to rebody a CF6. *IAL*

Below:

During 1935-8 the COA6 chassis had the AEC 7.7-litre engine in A171 indirect-injection form, although the proportions of the chassis were much as applied to the 8.8-litre version. The two large access holes in the bonnet side followed standard AEC practice of the time, but the decorative style of the grille between them on this 1938 example was quite similar to that on Daimler Straight Eight cars of the time. Coventry's 205, registered CWK 205, was based on chassis 10269 and was the last of a batch of 27, mostly with Brush 55-seat bodywork as here. This particular bus was painted in a reversed version of the operator's maroon and cream livery. *IAL*

Right:
Trent Motor Traction Co was one of two BET companies to favour Daimler COG5 buses for part of its fleet requirements in the late 1930s. The front-entrance double-decker was standard in several fleets in the district at the time; No 1056 (RC 6005) on chassis 10320 was one of 15 with Weymann bodies of composite construction using this layout, and dated from early 1938.
G. H. F. Atkins

position of Chief Engineer, not having Board status, was taken by Cyril M. Simpson, who had joined Daimler in 1919 and was to retain the post until the early 1960s. Bus design work was the responsibility of L. E. Clubb.

Appointed adviser after a decision to enter the trolleybus market early in 1936 was F. A. Garrett, hitherto with Leyland (and, before that, Ransomes in a similar capacity).

Above:
Daimler came a little too late to the trolleybus business to make much impact against by then well-established competitors. Its single major prewar success, in the sense of becoming the main type of vehicle operated, was at West Hartlepool — No 1 (EF 6701) of the new fleet, on chassis 20003, is seen in May 1938, posed outside the premises of Charles H. Roe Ltd, which built the bodies on the 14 CTM4 vehicles supplied. The revised style of rear hub, with slightly larger cylindrical cover, was also adopted for Daimler buses from about the same date. *AATC*

Left:
In contrast to the fast-growing successes in the Midlands and further north, Daimler had failed to secure a foothold for its buses among municipal fleets in more southerly parts of England until Swindon Corporation placed an order for six COG6 models with Park Royal 54-seat metal-framed bodies, delivered in the spring of 1938. This view of No 27 (BHR 453) on chassis 10374 shows the longer bonnet needed to accommodate the 6LW engine, the bulkhead being moved back by 7³⁄₁₆in compared to the COG5. Although these were to be Swindon's only examples of the type, deliveries of the postwar equivalent CVG6 would continue until 1967. *AATC*

At that time, many British tramway systems were being replaced by trolleybuses, and most of the major motorbus builders were already offering trolleybuses derived from their existing models. Daimler introduced the CTM4 two-axle trolleybus chassis (broadly equivalent to the COG5, but with the traction motor under the floor, air brakes, and suitably modified frame) and the CTM6 with three axles; the 'M' signified Metropolitan-Vickers electrical equipment, adopted as standard. New chassis number series began at 20001 for the CTM4 and 21001 for the CTM6, these prototypes eventually going respectively to the South Shields and Newcastle fleets.

It may have been the hoped-for expansion of business that led to the bus and trolleybus side of the Daimler business being transferred to a new BSA subsidiary, given the curiously awkward title Transport Vehicles (Daimler) Ltd, later in 1936. As it turned out, Daimler paid the penalty of being late on the scene with its trolleybus venture, for existing builders, notably AEC, Leyland, Karrier, Guy and Sunbeam, were all well established in this market by then. Only 25 Daimler trolleybuses were built up to 1939, the largest customer being West Hartlepool with 14 CTM4, Derby having six of the same type, while two CTM6 were sold to Belfast in 1938.

Meanwhile bus business continued to bound ahead, Birmingham taking further large COG5 batches, ending with 130 for delivery in 1939 (these last had FOF registrations, curiously apt for COG5 buses, for that, repeated, was not unlike the exhaust sound of examples of the period).

Above:
South Africa was Daimler's main export market for its buses in the late 1930s. Home-market restrictions on length and width did not apply, and an 18ft 9in-wheelbase single-deck chassis was introduced, suitable for vehicles of 30ft length and 8ft width. These two COG5 examples seen before shipping were fitted with 39-seat bodywork by Park Royal for service with Benoni Municipality, No 21, nearer the camera, being on chassis 8487. *IAL*

Right:
Export double-deckers were also being built to 8ft width. This COG6 (chassis number 10525) was the first to be supplied to Durban Corporation, seen posed after bodying at Park Royal in late 1938. *IAL*

Right:
The COG5/40 sold in modest numbers to independent operators, several choosing Willowbrook to build 39-seat bodywork to what became known as dual-purpose standard, being suitable for bus or coach duty. The compact bonnet and Willowbrook's seat design made such vehicles more comfortable than might have been expected, at least for people of medium height. This B & S example, No 232 (HL 9494) on chassis 8479 dating from May 1939, is seen at Leeds bus station in postwar years with body rebuilt, possibly by Barnaby of Hull. It passed to West Riding in 1950, and remained in service until 1953. *Don Morris/TWMC*

Above:
By 1939, Newcastle Corporation had built up the largest fleet of COG5 models outside Birmingham, comprising 71 double-deckers. The first three of the final batch of 20, dating from June of that year and led by No 222 (HTN 222) on chassis 10897, are seen here outside the premises of Northern Coachbuilders Ltd in Claremont Road, Newcastle, where the bodies had been built; 15 more were delivered later in the year, the remaining two being bodied by the (quite unrelated) Northern Counties Motor & Engineering Co, of Wigan. *Newcastle-upon-Tyne City Libraries*

In all, Birmingham had taken delivery of 841 COG5 buses (796 double-deckers and 45 single-deckers) in the period from 1934 to early 1940, a near-monopoly of its motorbus needs until 1938-9 when Leyland secured orders for 135 of its TD6c model with torque-converter transmission. Over that same period, the COG5 had also become the main type of double-deck bus placed in service by municipal fleets in Derby (with 26), Luton (21), Newcastle (71), Northampton (27), Stockton (22), Sunderland (30), West Hartlepool (17) and Wolverhampton (48), plus lesser totals in Aberdare, Belfast and South Shields. Following its introduction in late 1935, the COG6 (in some cases chosen along with COG5/40 single-deckers) was similarly the main choice in Aberdeen (28), Bradford (34), Dundee (30), Edinburgh (43), SHMD (34) and West Bromwich (36). Batches of COG6 were also supplied to Glasgow (25), Rochdale (15), Oldham (6) and Swindon (6), albeit in these cases in a minority among larger fleets of AECs and/or Leylands.

An important new customer was secured early in 1939, when Manchester Corporation, hitherto favouring locally-built Crossleys but with a growing share of Leylands, placed an impressive first order for 83 COG5, soon followed by 33 more, following some astute lobbying by Daimler sales staff largely on the basis of their locally-produced Gardner engines; delivery of these buses was, however, curtailed by wartime events.

There were small numbers of independent users, mainly bus operators, among which Venture, of Consett, was noteworthy, turning to the COG5/40 for nine buses and six coaches after receiving Gardner-engined Albions. The hold on the independent coach market of the CF6 era had all but vanished, Tailby & George being among the few others to favour the COG5/40 as a coach.

Export business was more encouraging, with South Africa as a very strong market for the COG6 — in addition to the Cape Town and Port Elizabeth fleets, there were 35 for Johannesburg and 36 for Durban. There were 70 COG5 double-deckers for the Bombay Electrical Supply & Tramways Co in 1937-9, with four of this chassis type but with single-deck bodies for China Motor Bus, Hong Kong, in 1936. Among single-deck models, New Zealand operator Chambers took four COG5 in 1935, with repeat orders each year up to 1939. In South Africa, there were orders from Pietermaritzburg and Springs for COG5 single-deckers, but Durban was noteworthy as a recipient in 1939-40 of 11 of a type designated COG6/40, these being on chassis with 18ft 9in wheelbase, and longer than permissible in Britain at the time — many export vehicles were wider as well as longer than those for home-market fleets.

5. War — Daimler in the Front Line

Contrary to widespread present-day belief, British preparations against the risk of a further war with Germany had begun well before the outbreak of hostilities in September 1939. Air Ministry discussions on mass production of aero engines, in which Geoffrey Burton as BSA Chairman and other motor industry leaders took part in May 1936, led to the shadow factory schemes under which participants ran Government-financed works as offshoots of their normal activities. Daimler's first shadow factory, alongside the Radford works, came into operation in 1937 and, with other premises often dispersed well away from Coventry, 50,800 Bristol radial aero engines and many other items were produced.

More closely related to Daimler's normal products were the armoured cars. Early in 1938, the Army asked Daimler to develop an armoured scout car intended mainly for reconnaissance, and by September a prototype had been built. It was to be able to negotiate ditches, ford rivers, climb gradients of up to 1 in 2 and yet travel at speed on ordinary roads. It used a six-cylinder petrol engine much as used in the then new 2½-litre car, of which a sporting version called the Dolphin was being driven in rallies to

good effect by Bob Crouch, in postwar years to become Daimler's Bus Sales Manager. The scout car had a fluid flywheel and preselective gearbox with separate reverse, allowing use of five speeds in forward or reverse, and all-round independent suspension; despite its 3-ton weight, something of the Dolphin's sporting character seems to have rubbed off, with talk of 'lap records on any roundabout'. The first quantity order was placed in May 1939, delivery commencing in December — ultimately some 6,665 were built.

Deliveries of bodied Daimler buses had been running at not far short of 500 per year in 1937-8, the figure dropping slightly to about 400 in 1939 but then more sharply to around half that in 1940. The first four examples of an additional COG5 variant had appeared in the last weeks of peacetime, these being COG5/60 buses with Brush bodywork, built to meet a Coventry Corporation requirement for 60-seat capacity, which posed some problems because of the 26ft length and 10½-ton gross weight limits then in force. The chassis, numbered 10827-30, had the same type of front end as the COG5/40 single-decker, thus making it just possible to squeeze in 31 rather upright seats in the

lower deck with a rearward-facing row of five at the bulkhead; the upper deck had seats for 29, this layout helping to meet tilt-test requirements despite the lighter chassis. Bodied, the unladen weight was 6 tons 9cwt 3qr. A further 17 similar buses followed in the period up to November 1940. Coventry received five additional 60-seat buses from November 1939 to January 1940, but these were on COA6 chassis, for which Metro-Cammell had developed a body light enough to bring the weight down to 6 tons 6cwt despite the heavier chassis, these having 31 seats upstairs and 29 below.

Bus chassis production continued fairly normally, if at a more modest rate than in peacetime, until the autumn of 1940 — there were even some instances of exports, although other buses intended for overseas operators were held and later diverted for home-market use as the war situation worsened and Britain stood alone after the fall of France in June 1940. Delivery of COG5 chassis for Manchester began in November 1939, these receiving bodies to that undertaking's Streamline design. This work was still in hand when Coventry began to be hit by a series of air raids in the autumn of 1940. On the night of 14 November, the Radford works was severely damaged in a huge raid on the city — this lasted 11 hours, causing a heavy death toll and destroying Coventry Cathedral among hundreds of buildings. There were direct hits on the bus assembly shop, destroying several Manchester chassis and badly damaging others. The net result was that only 71 of that undertaking's first order for 83 COG5 chassis were delivered, and the only two completed from the second order for 33 were built up after the bombing by combining good components from several chassis. Effectively, bus production had been brought to a halt, though three final COG5 double-decker chassis were assembled for works transport use in 1941, being given chassis numbers 11301-3 following 130 blanks left by other unfulfilled orders.

Right:

Only eight new Daimler single-deckers, all of the COG5/40 type, reached home-market customers in 1940. Allen's of Mountsorrel, Leicestershire, No 30 (BUT 741) was one of these; chassis 8543 was despatched to Willowbrook for construction of the 39-seat body just after the war began, in September 1939, and was delivered to the operator in February 1940. It was well cared for, being one of two such vehicles added to the fleet of Barton Transport when Allen's was taken over in 1955, and was retained for several more years. *Don Morris/TWMC*

Below:

The COG5 buses for Manchester Corporation formed a major part of work in hand in 1940. Seen here in an official picture, taken before wartime headlamp masks or white markings were applied, is No 1308 (GNA 456) on chassis 10975, which left Radford in April and entered service on 1 June, just as the war situation was worsening. The 54-seat body was built by English Electric to the operator's 'Streamline' specification, as already applied to Crossley and Leyland buses, though the cab as modified to suit the COG5's sloping-radiator chassis produced a particularly harmonious effect. They were popular buses, establishing Manchester as a major Daimler customer. *R. Marshall collection*

Above:
The morning of 15 November 1940 revealed horrific destruction in Coventry following one of the worst air raid attacks made on British targets during the whole war period. In the midst of the smoking ruins of the buildings in Broadgate were the mangled and largely burnt-out remains of Coventry Corporation No 240, one of the COG5/60 buses then less than a year old. It was one of six of the fleet's Daimlers that appeared to be beyond repair after the raid. A mile or so away at the Radford works there had been several direct hits on the bus chassis assembly shop, where numbers of COG5 models for Manchester were destroyed. *Imperial War Museum*

Right:
Bus chassis of that era were tough, although there may well have been an element of the 'won't be beaten' spirit in the Coventry municipal workshop staff's rebuilding of No 240 so that it could be sent back to Brush to receive a new body, to wartime 'utility' specification — it was back in service in December 1942, being one of four of the six buses badly damaged in the 14 November raid similarly rebuilt. As it happened, 240 was one of the buses chosen to receive development versions of the new Daimler CD6 engine in 1945, and remained in service until 1955. *TWM*

Above:
Three COG5 double-deckers were built as Daimler staff buses, these entering service after bodying by Willowbrook in May 1941. They were assembled largely from parts salvaged after the November 1940 bombing, and this view of EVC 947, on chassis 11301, shows evidence of that in the form of the front mudguards, which are of the special type (deeper and more rounded than the COG5 standard) specified for the Manchester orders. It is seen after sale to Worth's of Enstone, Oxfordshire, which acquired all three. *Don Morris/TWMC*

Below:
Eight COG5 models to export 18ft 9in wheelbase with Weymann bodywork of 30ft length and 8ft width, intended for Southern Rhodesia, were diverted in 1941, seven going to the Potteries fleet and one, on chassis 8493, becoming No 6 (EAX 728) with the West Monmouthshire Transport Board, a small municipal fleet. The bus ran until 1960, having received an AEC engine in 1956. *Don Morris/TWMC*

Right:
Five COG6 chassis to 8ft-wide export specification were delivered to Metro-Cammell in 1940 — this one (chassis 11154) in May of that year — and bodied for export to the Johannesburg municipal fleet. The worsening war situation prevented shipment, and in 1942 they were allocated for use in Britain despite not conforming to British dimensions, being given special dispensation. Four went to Birmingham City Transport, that shown becoming 1322 (FVP 922); it is seen as delivered in wartime grey livery. It seems that their design made quite a good impression — many postwar Birmingham buses had the 6LW engine, and the more sharply-raked windscreen was also adopted, having been found to minimise reflections from interior lights. *AATC*

There were similar blanks in the single-deck series, with 8568, a COG5/40 for Chambers of New Zealand sent to the packers for export in April 1940, as the highest number built, though allocations ran to 8590.

In all, 1,393 COG5 double-deck chassis had been built as such, including the 21 COG5/60 for Coventry; there were 412 COG6 and 100 COA6, making a total of 1,905 CO-prefix double-deck chassis, excluding conversions. There were 429 COG5 single-decker models (including COG5/40 types), 10 COS4 and 11 export COG6/40. Hence the overall total of oil-engined models built as such from 1933 to 1941 was 2,355, of which 2,245 had Gardner engines, easily exceeding the combined total of all petrol-engined bus models built by Daimler at Coventry.

Despite the air raids, the design and engineering staff had been working long hours during the autumn and winter of 1940-1 on a larger armoured car weighing 7 tons, in effect scaled up from the scout car, using a 4-litre 100bhp petrol engine and noteworthy in having disc brakes well over a decade before they began to be adopted for high-performance cars; 2,734 were built. As it turned out, the first batch to be completed was destroyed during two further heavy air raids on Coventry in April 1941, which left about half the Daimler works wrecked. Also destroyed was a prototype COG6/6 six-wheeler (chassis 15001) intended as a demonstrator for Leicester, then operating AEC Renown six-wheelers. Three COG5/6 had been ordered for China General Omnibus, then running Renowns with 5LW engines, but these were not built.

It was at that stage that the policy of dispersal to sites well away from the main factory that had begun a year earlier came into its own, and assembly of the scout cars moved from Radford to J. C. Bamford's works at Uttoxeter and armoured cars to a textile factory of Courtaulds Ltd in Wolverhampton. Military output was vital and Geoffrey Burton was appointed Chairman of the Tank Board, being

succeeded as Chairman of Daimler in December 1941 by Sir Bernard Docker, the son of the former BSA Deputy Chairman, Dudley Docker, who had initiated BSA's acquisition of Daimler in 1910. Sir Bernard also became Managing Director of the BSA group in 1944.

The more general dispersal of war factories all over Britain contributed to the need for an adequate supply of new buses, and the Ministry of Supply, by then controlling the whole of industry, sanctioned a limited production programme for double-decker buses built to standardised 'utility' specifications and allocated by the Ministry of War Transport. At first, chassis manufacture was to be shared by Leyland and Guy, with initial orders for 500 each, but urgency of tank production made Guy the sole supplier when deliveries began to reach operators in mid-1942.

Daimler was not in a position to build 'unfrozen' buses from parts in stock as was done elsewhere, but five COG6 double-deckers intended for Johannesburg and eight COG5 18ft 9in-wheelbase single-deckers for Rhodesia were diverted: Birmingham received four COG6 and West Monmouthshire one COG6 and one COG5 single-decker, the rest of these going to the Potteries fleet. When Daimler put forward a scheme in March 1942 for renewed bus production, this was welcomed, the first such chassis being delivered in December of that year. The initial order was for 350 chassis, of which the first 100 were to be of type CWG5, the 'W' signifying 'wartime' in the manner then common, but the resemblance to the COG5 was obvious. Light alloy materials were largely reserved for aircraft, so there was wider use of cast iron for items such as the engine crankcase, increasing the 4-ton chassis weight of the COG5 by about 6cwt.

It came as a pleasant surprise amid the general talk of elimination of non-essential refinements on wartime products that the CWG5 retained the fluid flywheel and

Above:

The CWG5 chassis retained the design refinements of the COG5 in final standard form. All had bodywork built to the utility standard of the time, with angular outline, but Massey, which built 30 of the bodies, made a virtue of necessity with its bold styling. Coventry 322 (EKV 822), on chassis 11335, delivered in March 1943, is seen in 1955. The body had been rebuilt in the Corporation workshops in 1951, more opening windows being added. A CWA6-style bonnet side with larger access holes had also been fitted, but the appearance was otherwise largely as built. *TWM*

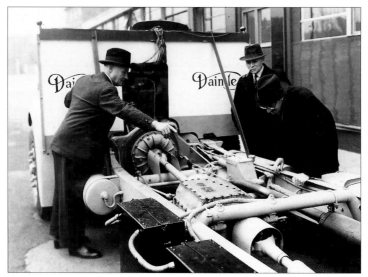

Left:

When it was announced in December 1942 that Daimler had resumed bus chassis production, there was understandable pride, and perhaps a little defiance, that this had proved possible after the severe air raid damage suffered in 1940 and 1941. It was no doubt also gratifying that the CWG5 model retained the (by then) traditional fluid flywheel and Wilson gearbox, both visible in this view. F. G. Couch, Director and Sales Manager of Transport Vehicles (Daimler), explains to Arthur Twidle of BET while Cyril Simpson, Daimler's Chief Engineer (with pipe), looks on. *IAL*

preselective gearbox and that the Gardner 5LW engine continued to be flexibly mounted. The only noticeable change in mechanical design was the adoption of a bought-in rear axle supplied by Kirkstall Forge of Leeds, identifiable by its domed hub caps, but even this was of basically similar underslung worm type to the Daimler-built unit used hitherto. Dimensionally and in appearance, the CWG5 was almost unchanged from its predecessor, including the 16ft 3⁵/₃₂in wheelbase, with only the painted finish for the radiator and the use of small military-style headlamps as identification points. The result was perhaps the most refined of all the 'utility' bus models from the passengers' viewpoint.

Resumption of bus chassis manufacture was quite a triumph after the hammering the Radford works had received in 1940-1 and there seemed to be a touch of defiance in Daimler's advertisement announcing its availability in December 1942, with 'Transport Vehicles (Daimler) Ltd, Coventry' set unusually boldly at its foot. In fact, although Radford was being rebuilt as quickly as possible, bus assembly had been moved temporarily to the Courtaulds factory in Wolverhampton.

The CWG5 chassis built were numbered 11304 to 11403, following on from the last COG5 double-deckers. Body construction to the utility specification of the time was divided between Duple, then at Hendon, and Massey Bros of Wigan, which each built 30 bodies to normal-height 'highbridge' pattern, and Brush at Loughborough, which contributed 40 of the 'lowbridge' type with sunken side gangway on the upper deck. This latter was far too many in terms of prewar Daimler production and, while the highbridge buses were doled out in very small numbers

mostly to regular Daimler users — Birmingham received a mere three, for example — the lowbridge buses often went to quite surprising customers not associated with the make, such as Red & White Services based at Chepstow (the largest recipient, with eight). The allocations of highbridge buses were on a geographic basis, Massey-bodied buses going to fleets in the north and Duple to those in the south, although Coventry's allocation of seven included examples of both.

From chassis number 11404, the chassis type became CWA6, it having been decided that AEC would be the main supplier of engines for wartime Daimler buses. Mechanically, they were very similar to the later COA6, using the A173 direct-injection version of the 7.7-litre engine. The appearance altered a little, with a coarse 'expanded-metal' radiator grille, much as used on military vehicles at the time, and a new one-piece pressing for its surround, though this retained the sloping profile hitherto associated with Gardner-engined models rather than the vertical form of the COA6. The A173 engine was more responsive than the 5LW and, with its preselective

Above:
The CWA6, with AEC 7.7-litre engine, followed on from the CWG5 as the standard wartime type; at the same time a new type of radiator shell was adopted, pressed in one piece and having a grille in 'expanded metal' which gave the appearance of wire mesh. This example, on chassis 11837, became Nottingham 68 (GTV 768) in October 1944. By then, Brush was building both highbridge and lowbridge bodies for the CWA6, this being an example of the former. It is seen outside Parliament Street depot in June 1950. *G. H. F. Atkins*

Right:
Representative of CWA6 models as originally supplied is Coventry Corporation 341 (EKV 941) on chassis 11638, delivered in February 1944. By this stage, Northern Counties was building a share of the highbridge double-deck output on the model, having gained permission to use its metal-framed construction instead of the composite construction laid down in the Ministry of Supply specification. *TWMC*

gearbox, the CWA6 could be quite a nimble performer in
town traffic. On the other hand, it was apt to seem fairly
noisy within, partly because of the rigid engine mounting,
but also because of the use of wooden slatted seats as part
of the 'utility' body specification from around mid-1943
until early 1945, when upholstered seats and other
improvements were again permitted.

Body contracts were more varied for the CWA6, though
Duple and Brush were the main suppliers, each of both
highbridge and lowbridge versions (these latter dropping
to about 10% of output), although Massey, Northern Counties, Park Royal, Roe and Weymann also all contributed
batches of highbridge bodies. By early 1944, the last of the
initial 250 of the type were entering service, and the next
order, for 480, was being completed as the war in Europe
was ending in June 1945, the final chassis number of this
batch being 12133. The MoS production system continued
for the first months of peacetime, the final example covered being 12675, a CWA6 supplied to Canvey & District
in April 1946, although limited numbers of further varia-
tions, some described below, were included within that
range of numbers.

The utility CWA6 buses were supplied to numerous
operators all over Britain, the production rate building up
to over 400 per year by the end of the war, much the same
as had applied in 1939, which was quite an achievement in
the circumstances, though becoming easier as the Radford
works came back into commission. Allocations were a
little more rational than had applied with the CWG5, most

going to urban fleets, among which peacetime users of
both Daimler and AEC buses with preselective gearboxes
were prominent, notable among the latter being London
Transport which revived the 'D' classification previously
used for the Daimler CC buses of 1913.

A new development was the introduction of a Daimler
diesel engine, the CD6. Work on this had begun under the
direction of Cyril Simpson in 1936, reaching the stage of
a prototype engine, but had been put aside on the outbreak
of war, the engine, drawings and test records being lost
in the bombing. Work was resumed in 1943 and further
test engines built before production began, at first on a
small scale. It was of 8.6-litre swept volume, the six cylinders having 4½in by 5½in bore and stroke. Some features
suggested both Gardner and Leyland influence, although
the cavity in the pistons had a shallow yet rounded cross-
section different from either; use of rear-end timing gears

Above:
Park Royal joined the firms bodybuilding on Daimler chassis under the wartime arrangements at the end of 1944, the principal recipient of such buses being Birmingham City Transport. No 1456 (FOP 456) on chassis 12158, delivered in August 1945, was one of 25 CWA6 models; it is seen after receiving a chromium-plated radiator shell, as was standard practice as part of subsequent refurbishment of such buses in this fleet. The first six CWD6 models, also for Birmingham, had similar bodywork. *F. W. York*

Below:
This picture of a CWD6 chassis accompanied press announcements of the model in May 1945. Apart from the Daimler CD6 engine, it shows the form in which chassis were being delivered just before the war ended, with small military-style headlamps, both being masked — these proved more effective than they looked once the masks were removed. This chassis has the expanded-metal grille although CWD6 models were normally fitted with a vertically-slatted version, suggesting it might have been a prototype or one of the earliest built. *IAL*

was claimed to give more accurate fuel injection timing but made attention to them more difficult.

The first CD6 engines had been fitted to one or more of Daimler's own 1941 COG5 buses (chassis 11301-3) by about February 1945 and another very early one fitted by March to one of the Coventry COG5/60 buses, No 240 with chassis 11045. This latter acted as a testbed installation, although three others were also fitted to COG5/60 buses, all four then retaining CD6 engines until withdrawal.

The first six examples of the new CWD6 chassis with the CD6 engine were chassis 12065-7 and 12074-6, completed in February-March 1945 and supplied to the Birmingham municipal fleet in May-June; further examples were thereafter interspersed in production with CWA6 models, London Transport receiving 168 CWA6 and 13 CWD6 as its allocation, for example. The CWD6 chassis reverted to the Daimler-built rear axle, the CWA6 generally continuing with the Kirkstall unit. Later, as production of the

Above
Most Daimler bus chassis built in the first peacetime months up to early 1946 continued to be CWA6 models. London Transport enlarged its fleet of such buses during this period and D173 (HGF 800) on chassis 12567, new in March 1946, was one of 37 in Green Line livery for the Romford services. The bodywork was by Duple, by far the largest producer of bodies for this model. They were rather austere to be regarded as 'coaches' and were taken off this duty in 1951. D173 is seen at Aldgate in company with trolleybus 1469, one of the 'chassisless' Metro-Cammell-AEC vehicles built in 1939-40. *IAL*

Daimler axle built up, a further sub-variant, the CWA6D, combined this with the AEC engine. Manchester Corporation had not added any utility buses to its fleet until the 43 Daimlers 'owed' as a result of the Radford works bombing of November 1940 materialised as CWA6D models with Brush bodywork to relaxed utility design, placed in service between December 1945 and March 1946.

New postwar models were introduced but the CWA6 and CWD6 double-deck models continued in small-scale production into the early postwar years. In particular, London Transport decided to order 100 further CWA6 chassis (12810-12909) fitted with Park Royal bodies to a transitional design built later in 1946, bringing its total of D class Daimlers to 281. It seems probable that other late examples were instances of using up stocks of parts, the highest-numbered CWD6, 13541, leaving the factory in August 1947 and entering service with Derby Corporation in January 1948. In all, there were 100 CWG5, 1,238 CWA6 and 185 CWD6.

6. 'Victory' and a Broader Market

The end of World War 2 brought a huge need for fleet renewal in the bus- and coach-operating industries, wartime supplies falling far short of the norm. Orders for post-war delivery had come from some operators during the war, turning into a torrent as hostilities ceased. There was also a general atmosphere of relief, and a wish to escape from wartime austerity.

A touch of 'swords into ploughshares' was evident in the use of the 4.095-litre six-cylinder petrol engine first used in the armoured car for the Daimler DC27 ambulance introduced in 1946 — in this form it developed 105bhp at 3,600rpm. The chassis, with coil-sprung independent front suspension and, of course, fluid flywheel transmission, was derived from that of the DE27 limousine, with wheelbase extended to 12ft 6in and offset final drive. The London County Council had adopted a policy of using refined car models as a basis for its prewar ambulance fleet, its Talbots having served the capital well in wartime, but the new Daimlers of the early postwar years must rank among the most luxurious public ambulance fleets ever operated. Hertfordshire County Council was also a user. The chassis number series 54000-54499 indicates a build sanction of 500 — the model remained in production into the early 1950s, when awareness of rising costs turned health authorities to more utilitarian types of vehicle.

A new range of bus chassis was put in hand in 1945 to succeed the CW series and, with 'Victory' much in the air, it was given the prefix CV. With the Daimler CD6 8.6-litre engine in production, it was natural to promote the CVD6 as the standard model, but the Gardner LW types continued to be available in the CVG5 and CVG6, all of these built in both double- and single-deck forms, with wheelbase of

16ft 3⁵⁄₂in and 17ft 2½in respectively, plus a 19ft export single-deck option. The AEC 7.7-litre A173 continued to be available and thus there was also a CVA6, though only built as a double-decker. The CV-series chassis were similar in mechanical specification to the previous generations of Daimler bus models, with fluid flywheel and four-speed preselective gearbox as the only transmission option. A choice of vacuum-hydraulic or triple-servo brakes was offered, the latter tending to come back into favour in the industry at the time.

The key CV-series feature was a new frame, with the front portions of the sidemembers parallel to each other over the front axle instead of tapering inwards from the mid-section all the way to the front dumb-irons, as on previous models. The front ends of the frame sidemembers were hidden by a pair of quite prominent rounded covers, one each side of the radiator, giving a characteristic look. The radiator itself, though retaining the pressed form of shell, now had a vertical front face, and this had the effect of slightly reducing the distance between radiator and bulkhead, which became 4ft 6in as standard. The exception was the CVG6, where part of the extra engine length was now accommodated by moving the radiator forward by about 3in, the bulkhead moving rearwards a similar amount instead of by over 7in as on the COG6.

A prototype single-deck chassis to CVD6 specification was built during 1945, but the first examples of the new series built for sale were part of an order for 20 CVG6 double-deck models for South Africa; there were also six CVG5 for Bombay. Permission was given for them to be built under the Ministry of Supply allocation system then still in force, and they had chassis numbers interspersed

Above
Daimler's DC27 ambulance model of 1946 was adopted by the London County Council as the basis for re-equipping its war-ravaged fleet. The standard body was built by Barker, normally associated with luxurious cars. The front-end styling was quite adventurous at that date in using only a stylised echo of the Daimler radiator in the fluted strip at the top of the grille — an idea taken up on bus models from 1952. *AATC*

Left:
The DC27 ambulance chassis borrowed from bus practice in having an offset transmission line, the casing for the hypoid-bevel rear axle being positioned to allow a 1ft 9in gangway level. The 4-litre six-cylinder petrol engine was basically as used in the wartime armoured car. *IAL*

among the later utility CWA6 models; the first, with chassis number 12414, left Radford works in December 1945 for bodying by Weymann before shipping to Cape Town. When the MoS era ended with CWA6 chassis 12675, Daimler reverted to its practice of issuing chassis numbers on receipt of order, and reservations ran ahead astonishingly quickly, some operators placing bulk orders for delivery over several years. The actual order of build was often very different due to the widely varying circumstances applying.

Deliveries of CVD6 chassis began with single-deck examples in April 1946, the first to be completed, 13010, going to Venture of Consett which had placed a remarkable order for 48, almost enough to replace that firm's entire fleet as it then stood. They had Willowbrook bodywork to a neat-looking bus design that was also favoured by several other independent operators of the CVD6. Double-deck CVD6 models followed later in the year as the CWD6 faded from the scene, but did not reach operators in any numbers until 1947, Aberdeen and Dundee being among early recipients. The CVA6 also entered production from April 1946, before the last CWA6 batches were completed, Belfast being the first user with a batch of 40.

There was a noticeable delay before postwar home-market Gardner-engined Daimlers began to come through, the first such chassis not leaving the factory until January 1947, although further batches of CVG6 for South Africa and CVG5 for Bombay, doubtless given priority in the Government's drive for exports, had been built in 1946. Gardner engines, whose good reputation for economy and reliability had broadened as a result of the war, were in strong demand, and this sometimes delayed construction. There was quite a widespread tendency for operators which had favoured the COG5 prewar to switch to the CVG6 for their postwar double-deckers. Apart from coping with heavier vehicles, there was also a growing trend towards using larger engines to give greater reliability and longer life. These arguments could be applied to the CD6

engine, which also had the virtue of quiet and smooth running, but it was at first regarded as an unknown quantity against the proven Gardner and its acceptance remained patchy, especially among the larger fleets. For a time, the CVA6 had a rather broader following than the COA6 in prewar days, with Belfast, Birmingham, Liverpool and Western SMT, as well as Coventry, taking batches.

An approximate analysis of the quantities of different types in the period up to 1950 reveals that, among double-deck models, there were roundly 1,130 CVG6, 800 CVD6, 370 CVG5 and 325 CVA6, as well as late examples of the CW series as mentioned in the last chapter and smaller numbers of types yet to be described. Among single-deckers the position was more standardised, with about 690 CVD6, 95 CVG5 and 41 CVG6, these last-mentioned introduced to meet the requirements of the Huddersfield undertaking for its hilly terrain, though a batch was also supplied to Salford. Thus the CVG6 was now the most popular double-deck model, although outnumbered at that stage by the CVD6 if both double- and single-deck types were included. The total bus chassis production rate over that period averaged about 750 per year.

Manchester thought highly of its COG5 models of 1940-1 and chose the directly-equivalent CVG5 for its first 100 postwar Daimlers, although that undertaking's early adoption of 8ft width instead of the then usual 7ft 6in

meant that the 5LW engines had to work hard to cope with the 8-ton unladen weight — the CVG6 was specified for subsequent Manchester batches. The CVG5 double-decker became a rarity in Britain in this period, but was exported in quite large numbers, mainly for Bombay, although Kowloon received some in 1949.

The more common switch from COG5 to standardisation on the CVG6 was signalled by the delivery of chassis number 13737, the first to arrive of a batch of 20 for Northampton in May 1947; as it turned out, that municipality was then to remain loyal to the type until it ceased production in 1968. Other COG5 users to buy CVG6 models included Newcastle, Sunderland, West Hartlepool and Wolverhampton, while Swindon went from COG6 to CVG6. New recruits to the CVG6 included the Maidstone and Newport municipalities, with small batches. A much larger-scale new CVG6 user proved to be Salford, placing orders for 195 CVG6 with Metro-Cammell bodies, delivered in 1950-2.

The situation in the Midlands was more complex. Choice of chassis type at Birmingham seems to have been influenced at least partly by delivery prospects. The first 75 postwar Daimlers were on CVA6 chassis and, in a sense, this batch could be compared to London's 100 CWA6 of 1946 — the chassis numbers followed on and chassis delivery was not far behind, although Birmingham not only opted for the CV-series chassis but also specified flexible engine mountings, not standard for AEC-engined Daimlers.

Below:
The strong demand for new coaches led to delays at established bodybuilders as they struggled to cope, and this led to several ventures into construction by newcomers to the industry. Among them was Yorkshire Yachtbuilders, of Bridlington, which built batches of bodies on CVD6 chassis for dealers Holdsworth & Hanson, which found customers for them mainly in the North of England. Among the latter was W. Robinson & Sons of Great Harwood, Lancs, the vehicle shown being JTC 34 on chassis 15083, one of three for the fleet from a batch of 11 chassis bodied by this firm in 1948. *TWMC*

Lower right:
Despite Daimler's understandable efforts to promote its own engine, the CVG6 with Gardner 6LW proved the most popular choice for double-deckers in the postwar years. This example, West Hartlepool Corporation No 56 (EF 8558), with Roe 56-seat body, was exhibited at the Commercial Motor Show in October 1948, being distinguished by non-standard gold lining-out. It was 8ft wide and was the first of an order for 24 with chassis numbers 14548-71, although the last 15 of these were not built until 1953. *TWMC*

Left:
A goodwill and trade promotion trip to Copenhagen in 1948 led to the assembly of this remarkable line-up of municipal double-deckers in Daimler's works yard. All but one were new CVD6 models, the exception being the Glasgow CWD6 (second from left) dating from September 1945 but spruced up for the occasion — that authority had some CVD6 on order but not yet delivered. From left to right are: Nottingham 278 (KTV 278) on chassis 14777; Glasgow 157 (DUS 463) on 12343; SHMD 40 (KMA 510) on 14924; Birmingham 1822 (HOV 822) on 13979; Bradford 546 (EKY 546) on 14858, and Salford 345 (CRJ 345) on 15013. Brush was building bodies for several operators on CVD6 chassis at around this time, using a timber-framed design derived from its wartime utility type (as found on the Glasgow bus) and seen here on the first, third and fifth buses in this line-up. The Birmingham and Salford buses were bodied by Metro-Cammell. Despite the gloomy day, it must have been a colourful sight, with Glasgow's orange and green, together with Bradford's light blue and Birmingham's very dark blue and cream offsetting the darker greens of Nottingham, SHMD and Salford. *TWMC*

Completed buses did not begin to arrive until mid-1947;
the well-finished bodies were to Birmingham's postwar
specification, and the end result was a very refined bus,
perhaps the quietest of any model having the 7.7-litre AEC
engine, though the 8-ton unladen weight rather limited performance. Then came 75 CVG6, followed by a split order
for 88 CVD6 and 87 CVG6 before the choice came down
in favour of the CVD6 for 100 buses delivered in 1949-50.
At Coventry, the AEC engine tradition was continued
through the choice of the CVA6 with Metro-Cammell
body for the first 96 postwar buses, these being quite similar to the Birmingham buses in outline but seating 60
and built to a slightly less elaborate specification, retaining
the 'solid' engine mountings, for example. Although the
first seven chassis (12693-9) preceded Belfast's numerically, they were not delivered until 1948. At West Bromwich, the CVG6 became the standard postwar double-deck
choice, although there were six CVD6 in 1948.

The CVD6 tended to be the Daimler model chosen by
smaller undertakings or those where fleet deliveries were
divided between several suppliers. The type did quite
well for a time in Scotland, where Glasgow had 43 single-
deckers and then 65 double-deckers in 1948-51 when AEC
and Albion were regarded as main suppliers. Aberdeen
split orders between the CVD6 and AEC until 1950-1,
when 35 CVG6 were supplied. At Dundee the position was
rather similar, although there the CVD6 remained in
favour until 1953. At Edinburgh, the CVD6 was chosen for
16 buses in 1948-9, with 10 CVG5 single-deckers, but the
main postwar delivery was of 62 CVG6 with Birmingham-
style Metro-Cammell bodies in 1949-50. In England, Derby
standardised on the CVD6 from 1947 to 1952 and another
Midlands success was at Leicester, where 30 CVD6 were
added to a largely AEC and Leyland fleet in 1948-9.

Although quite a number of BET companies had taken
CWA6 double-deckers, only Potteries took a batch of 10
CVD6 single-deck buses in the early postwar period.
There was more success with Scottish company fleets,
notably with the same model in coach form, of which
Alexander placed 35 with Burlingham bodies in service in
1947-9. The 30 Western SMT CVA6 buses were joined in
1950-1 by 30 CVG6 which had been ordered by Young's
of Paisley, by then taken over; the latter had others in its
fleet and its Paisley & District subsidiary had five CVG5.

The potential of the CVD6 as a coach was soon realised
by independent operators and about 380 of the type —
roughly half the total production over the 1946-50 period
— received bodywork of this type, most being sold to
independent operators. Many were bodied by Duple,
Burlingham and Plaxton but sizeable numbers went to
smaller bodybuilders such as Heaver, Wilks & Meade and
Yorkshire Yachtbuilders. One operator, Ernie Hartness, of
Skelton, near Penrith, coped with bodybuilding delays by
fitting 21 out of 30 new CVD6 chassis with a variety of

Top:
Africa continued to be a good market for Daimler buses. Three CVD6 double-deck chassis (16936-8) were exported to Kumasi Town Council, in the Gold Coast, in February 1949, and it is thought that the locally-built body shown was fitted to one of them; the other two, as well as several CVD6 single-deck chassis, had dual-doorway single-deck bodies of similarly sturdy wood-framed construction. *IAL*

Above:
The production of long-wheelbase export chassis resumed after the war, this version being designated CVG5XSD. Weymann built the metal-framed 39-seat body on eight examples built in 1948 for Salisbury Municipality in what was then Southern Rhodesia. *IAL*

Left:
Coventry added 96 CVA6 models with Metro-Cammell 60-seat bodywork to its fleet in 1948-50, continuing the ideas developed in 1939, although they were not of lightweight construction. No 23 (FHP 23), on chassis 13430, was delivered in August 1948 and is seen here in Broadgate in June 1963 with the surviving spire of the old cathedral still dominating the scene; at that date some of the temporary buildings erected after the 1940 bombing were still in place. *TWM*

Below:
Huddersfield Corporation, operating in a hilly area, was keen to continue its policy of standardising on the Gardner 6LW engine for its single-deck fleet, which had been based on AEC chassis with fluid transmission prewar but not offered postwar. Daimler stepped into the breach, supplying 30 CVG6 single-deckers on which Willowbrook built 34-seat bodywork. No 94, on chassis 14938, was one of the final delivery, this bus being an Earls Court Show exhibit when new in October 1950. It is seen here in company with two of the fleet's AEC Regent III 9.6-litre double-deckers. *Don Morris/TWMC*

Above:
The CD650 was Daimler's answer to models from AEC and Leyland with engines of just under 10-litre capacity. The engine, also called CD650, was very similar in most design features to the CD6 but with the cylinder bore increased to 5in, which increased the swept volume to 10.6 litres. The chassis was also new, with a parallel-sided frame at the front which gave space for the wider radiator which was to be the model's most obvious feature. This view of a chassis under construction is thought to show the last of the initial batch of three, 16927, which became the 1948 Show exhibit, stripped of the temporary cab structure seen here. *IAL*

Left:
The first CD650 buses to go into service with a British operator were a pair supplied to Tailby & George Ltd, of Willington, near Derby, trading as Blue Bus Services, a committed Daimler customer since 1935. No DR14 (PRA 388), based on chassis 17658, is seen here in Derby bus station when new in April 1951. Willowbrook, less sure-footed with double-deck styles of body than with its single-deckers, produced a design which, through the narrowness of the cab, emphasised the width of the radiator. It remained in service until 1970; a pair of similar buses dating from 1953 were preserved. *G. H. F. Atkins*

Above:
Perhaps the most unusual use for a Daimler CVD6 was this mobile unit of Birmingham Post & Mail Ltd. Based on chassis 16910, it dated from July 1950 and contained a printing machine, together with a small dark room, to facilitate coverage of local events. The bodywork, by Wilsdon of Solihull, was doubtless intended to be eye-catching, yet seemed oddly flamboyant for use by the rather sober and well-respected *Birmingham Post*. *TWM*

second-hand bodies, often getting them into use within a week or two of delivery, and sometimes using double-deck chassis to carry bodies from short-wheelbase models — some were later sent to receive new Plaxton coach or Roe double-deck bodies.

In addition to standard CVG6 export models for South Africa and Australia, 20 of a six-wheeled version designated CVG6/6 and fitted with Weymann 66-seat bodies were delivered to the Cape Town Tramways fleet in 1949. These had air-pressure brakes and the rear bogie, made by Kirkstall, was common to the 92 postwar Daimler trolley-buses, all six-wheelers, of which Rotherham took 44 single-deckers of types CTE6 and CTC6 (with English Electric and Crompton electrical equipment respectively) in 1949-51, Glasgow received 30 CTM6 with Metro-Cammell bodies to London Transport style, and 18 CTM6 were exported to Pretoria, South Africa.

In 1948, Daimler introduced a new model, the CD650 double-decker, with 10.6-litre six-cylinder engine similarly named. It was meant as an answer to the 9.6-litre AEC Regent III and 9.8-litre Leyland PD2 already in production by then, yet its other main features — high-pressure hydraulic operation of brakes and epicyclic gearbox, and power-assisted steering — had been advocated in a wartime trade press article by Cyril Simpson, Daimler's Chief Engineer. A chassis was displayed at the Earls Court Show that year, readily distinguished by its unusually broad version of the distinctive Daimler radiator, though this was also used on the CVG6/6 six-wheelers.

Large orders for the CVG6 with Metro-Cammell bodywork were placed by Salford City Transport, the first being for 90 delivered in 1950-1. The body design, which became known as the Phoenix, showed Birmingham influence in the use of a straight staircase and other features, while having a more orthodox frontal appearance. No 351 (CRJ 351) on chassis 14572 was the first, delivered in April 1950. The horizontally-split bonnet side was a new feature. Salford found the deep radiator vulnerable to minor damage, and specified a shorter version on later deliveries. *IAL*

Sales of the CD650 proved to be slow and meagre: five were exported to Johannesburg at the end of 1949, but the first for use in Britain were a pair with lowbridge Willowbrook bodywork supplied to Tailby & George Ltd of Willington, near Derby, in spring 1951; two more followed in 1953. The largest fleet was a batch of six with East Lancs bodies built later in 1951 for Halifax Corporation, to whose hilly terrain the large engine was well suited, but the cost of keeping the hydraulic system serviceable proved a major problem, the power steering also being disliked for its lack of self-centring. In all, 24 double-deck chassis were built, the balance being made up of demonstrators and development chassis. A 20ft-wheelbase export single-deck version, having an air brake option, did very slightly better, with 39 sold. It seems that the technology employed in the CD650 was not sufficiently well developed — yet, a few years later, high-pressure hydraulic brakes were to prove very successful on London Transport's Routemaster.

Right
Rotherham Corporation's trolleybus system was one of the minority in Britain using an exclusively single-deck fleet for most of its existence, and by the later 1930s had a reputation for running the fastest trolleybus services in the country. At that time the emphasis was on six-wheelers of AEC, Guy and Sunbeam manufacture, but Daimler became the postwar supplier, with 26 CTE6 and 18 CTC6 in 1949-50, all with 38-seat centre-entrance bodywork of East Lancs design. Seen here is No 22 (FET 622) on chassis 15866, one of the CTC6 type dating from 1950; it was among those exported to Tranvias de Zarazoga for operation in Cadiz after some of the Rotherham routes were abandoned in 1955. *AATC*

Above:
As part of a change of policy following the route changes of 1955, Rotherham Corporation decided that 20 of its CTE6 trolleybuses should be rebodied by Roe as 70-seat rear-entrance double-deckers. This view of No 35 (FET 338), which had been numbered 78 as a single-decker and was based on chassis 15871 dating from 1949, shows it as newly in service in this form in May 1956. *R. Stapleton*

7. New Ideas but Harder Times

The year 1950 was one of change in British bus design, with revised legal dimensional limits and the turning point of a major change in single-deck layout. Yet the main new Daimler development to emerge at the time was a 'face-lift' planned for its own vehicles by an operator; as events turned out, it cloaked the ability of the CV-series double-decker to see off a succession of challengers.

Rather surprisingly, from 1950 the hitherto very conservative Birmingham City Transport adopted a new design of 'three-quarter-width' bonnet with coarsely-slatted grille, to be common to new buses being purchased from

Below:
The 'new look' bonnet and grille design developed by Birmingham City Transport was adopted for its deliveries of double-deckers of all makes from early 1950 to 1954. Examples from Crossley and Guy had entered BCT service in February and July 1950, but Daimler deliveries did not begin until September with No 2031, the first of 100 CVD6 with Metro-Cammell bodies to this style. It may have been a wish to reassert Daimler identity that led to the temporary addition of the 'eyebrows' motif — intended to suggest the top of a traditional Daimler radiator — on 2065 (based on chassis 15730) seen here when new in January 1951; BCT declined to accept the feature. *TWMC*

Crossley, Daimler and Guy. The latter by then had a pre-selective gearbox option and made a major revision to the design of its Arab model, later known as the Mark IV, to meet BCT ideas. This was to have the Gardner 6LW engine, and it proved just possible to accommodate this within the standardised bonnet design with a length of 5ft. The bonnet design was christened the 'new look' in line with a women's clothing fashion style of the time.

The first new-look Daimlers, on chassis numbered 15710-809, were 100 CVD6 which entered service with BCT from the autumn of 1950 to mid-1951, immediately followed by a further 150 of the same type in the period to March 1952. The new-look front was then offered as an option for other operators, Coventry being the first to adopt it for 40 buses delivered from December 1951 to the following autumn, also on CVD6 chassis. The new-look style was soon being adopted by a growing number of Daimler's customers.

By this time, the bus industry was coming under strong pressure to reduce costs as competition from cars began to grow, and fuel economy came under renewed attention. Despite its recent successes at Birmingham and Coventry, the CD6 engine was fast losing favour, partly because it

Above:
Manchester Corporation chose the CVG6 chassis for 90 buses delivered between September 1950 and July 1951. They had Metro-Cammell 58-seat bodywork to a design based on the Phoenix style as developed for Salford, but with conventional half-landing staircases and Manchester-style details. Seen here in November 1969 is 4152 (KND 913) on chassis 17078, followed by 3448 and 3575 — Leyland PD2 buses of 1956 and 1959 — plus a gaggle of assorted Minis. *TWM*

Left:
From 1950, Aberdeen Corporation had reverted to its prewar choice of Gardner 6LW engines for its Daimler double-deckers after favouring the CWD6 and CVD6 in 1946-8. No 32, based on chassis 16171, was one of 10 CVG6 with bodies built to Park Royal design by Brockhouse and supplied in 1951.
Stewart J. Brown

Left:
Changes in regulations allowed home-market single-deckers to be up to 30ft long from mid-1950, and small numbers of CVD6 coaches were built to this length. W. Alexander & Sons Ltd took delivery of 13 with Eastern Coach Works bodywork of the style normally associated with the Bristol LWL6B chassis. Only the subtly-altered shape of the front grille to suit the slightly taller CVD6 radiator conveyed the difference in chassis make and model. D47 (DMS 560) seen here was based on chassis 15271 and dated from June 1951.
R. F. Mack

couldn't match Gardner efficiency, heightened by the latter's K-series modifications of 1950. A drop in overall vehicle production also made Gardner engines less scarce. In addition, the CD6 sometimes proved more troublesome, although operators' experience varied considerably in this respect.

At the 1952 Show, Daimler introduced a new lightweight model, again largely in search of fuel economy. This was the CLG5, which used the 16ft 4in-wheelbase frame and the Lockheed power-hydraulic brake system introduced for the CD650 but with lightweight components and reverting to the 5LW engine. The first example, chassis 18334, received a prototype MCW Orion lightweight body and was exhibited before delivery to Potteries Motor Traction; a similar chassis, 18335, went to Birmingham with a light version of that operator's standard style of body. Although further examples were planned, including a CLD6 version with modified CD6 engine, subsequent development reverted to the CV-series designations — for a time it seemed as if 'L' and 'V' were being interpreted to

mean 'Lockheed' and 'Vacuum'. Operators preferred the triple-servo brakes by then standard on CV chassis, and the CL models never went into quantity production.

Another of the prototype light chassis, 18337, eventually emerged in 1954 as a CVG6 with light Northern Counties body, registered PHP 220. Meanwhile, a batch of eight light CVG5 double-deckers with Roe bodywork and traditional radiators had been supplied to Sunderland in summer 1953, and that undertaking adopted the CVG5, in new-look lightweight form, for 53 further buses up to 1958. Also built in 1953 were 10 standard CVG6 (15181-90) for Northampton, completing an earlier order, these having the traditional radiator and thought to be the last such batch, although the last few of a 100-bus order begun in 1952 for Belfast (98 CVG6 and 2 CVD6, numbered 18036-135) entered service early in 1954.

Following completion of the Belfast order, the new-look front became standard, and production of double-deckers concentrated on the CVG6 and, to some degree, the revived CVG5. The redesigned chassis adopted some features

Left:
The traditional style of front-engined half-cab single-decker fell rapidly from favour in Britain in the early 1950s. Among the last built were three for Lancaster Corporation on CVG5 chassis, fitted with Northern Counties bodywork, delivered in December 1952. This one, No 466 (NTF 466) on chassis 18003, has survived and was photographed in July 1977 when on a Morecambe seafront service, its longevity being linked to the Queen's own Silver Jubilee that year.
M. F. Haddon

Above:
Exports of CVD6 models continued on a limited scale into the 1950s. Kumasi Town Council took some complete with Saunders-Roe 40-seat bodywork to that concern's Rivaloy metal-framed design in 1951-2, this example being posed at Beaumaris Castle before delivery. *IAL*

Below:
Revived interest in weight-saving led to the development of the CLG5 model, reverting to the Gardner 5LW engine. It was offered only in 7ft 6in width and using 12-volt batteries. One of the first pair of chassis built for the Commercial Motor Show of 1952 is seen here. Some features of the design were derived from the CD650, including its power-hydraulic brake system and hydraulic gear-change operation. Somewhat ironically, the

chassis weight quoted — 4 tons 6cwt — was exactly the same as that of the wartime CWG5, originally considered quite heavy. *IAL*

Right:
The bodied 1952 Show exhibit CLG5 was chassis 18334, with the prototype Orion lightweight body built by Metropolitan-Cammell, developing the ideas embodied in its lightweight 60-seat bodies built for Coventry in 1939-40. The unladen weight of the complete bus was 6 tons 2cwt, a remarkably low figure mainly due to the body, unkindly described by one observer as 'skin and bones'. Potteries Motor Traction Co Ltd had been a customer for COG5 buses and was unusual among BET companies in maintaining ongoing contact with Daimler developments. *IAL*

from both the CD650 and the CL models, including the 16ft 4in wheelbase and the gate-type preselector control to the left of the steering column instead of the traditional Daimler quadrant on the right.

Demand for the Daimler engine fell right away and it was officially dropped in 1954. Birmingham had switched back to the CVG6 for two further, and final, batches of 125 each in 1952-4, ending at chassis 18288, these being noteworthy for having bodies built by Crossley (which by then had ceased chassis manufacture), albeit to the standard BCT new-look outline of the time. They completed a

major fleet renewal and tramway replacement programme begun in 1947, in which Daimler had been the largest (but by no means sole) chassis supplier; following this the undertaking purchased only two ex-demonstrator buses until 1961.

The cessation of Birmingham orders was a major factor in a big drop in Daimler's bus output in the later 1950s, although there was a general fall-off affecting the whole industry as demand dropped. Fortunately, orders from other users continued, even if at a slower rate than previously, and some important new customers were added.

Left:
In the event, the CLG5 failed to become a production model, although several operators took buses incorporating its lightweight features combined with more conventional triple-servo vacuum brakes. Walsall Corporation, by then under the management of R. Edgley Cox — well-known for his innovative ideas — took three buses reported to have been ordered as CLG5, but built as CVG5. The second of these was No 821 (TDH 673) on chassis 18667, seen arriving at Earls Court for the 1954 Show. It had 65-seat bodywork by Northern Counties — much less austere in finish than the Orion, but still creditably light at 6 tons 19cwt. *IAL*

Left:
Birmingham, although experimenting with lighter models, including the 1952 CLG chassis that had been on Daimler's stand, reverted to the CVG6 for 250 further 'new look' buses delivered in 1952-4 but switched to Crossley-built bodywork, which had impressed BCT far more than the chassis of that make. No 2851 (JOJ 851), on chassis 17864 and dating from November 1952, carried its age well as it paused at the traffic lights in Hill Street in July 1966. *TWM*

Above:
As the demand for buses fell, competition between manufacturers intensified. Rochdale Corporation had standardised on AECs from 1947 to 1952, so it was quite an achievement for Daimler to secure the double-deck order for 1953-4, with 30 CVG6 models delivered in two equal batches. Weymann supplied the bodywork and this undertaking continued to favour the elegant four-bay style shown, which suited the 'new look' chassis quite well. No 244 (JDK 744), on chassis 18308, was delivered in March 1953 and is seen against a typical local background of mill chimneys and moorland. *Don Morris/TWMC*

Manchester had adopted a policy of splitting orders between Leyland and Daimler in the 1950s, and took 90 CVG6 in 1953-5, the last 10 having lightweight bodies, followed later in 1955 by 20 CVG5, the first on a lightweight chassis, 40 more arriving in 1956-7. Another operator to be interested in the lightweight project was Walsall Corporation, by then under the management of R. Edgley Cox and always on the look-out for new ideas; three buses ordered as CLG5 materialised as CVG5. The Potteries Motor Traction fleet took 30 CVG5 models with lightweight bodies in 1956, this concern continuing as the only BET company to favour Daimler buses for part of its needs in this period.

A further effect of the general drive towards fuel economy was a tendency for the CVG6 to regain business lost to models such as the 9.6-litre AEC Regent III, an instance being Rochdale, with 30 CVG6 in 1953-4; Halifax and Glasgow also became CVG6 users, with 22 in 1954 and 50 in 1955 respectively. Another significant example was Leeds, traditionally largely an AEC stronghold, which received 20 CVG6 in 1955-6 and continued to favour the model for a share of most subsequent orders.

Meanwhile, there had been developments among single-deckers. A 30ft-long version of the CVD6 and CVG5 with 19ft wheelbase was introduced in 1950 to take advantage of the then new home-market length limit, users including Dundee with 10 such CVD6 in 1951, while the CVG5 in this long form was chosen by West Bromwich for five

buses in 1951-2. Small numbers of CVD6 30ft coaches were built, and here the newly-reintroduced five-speed gearbox option was useful. The first to enter service were probably a pair with Plaxton bodies for Hartness of Penrith dating from June 1950, but perhaps the best-known were the 13 for Alexander in 1951 which had ECW bodywork of the full-fronted style used on the Bristol LWL6B. Reaction to this variant was limited, mainly because purchasers of high-quality coaches were by then interested in the new mid-underfloor-engined models. Daimler did not decide to produce one until April 1950 (significantly just as the Leyland Royal Tiger was announced), which was too late for it to have anything ready for the 1950 Show.

The new chassis, with higher straight frame and CD650-style power-hydraulic brake system, was christened 'Free-line' — the first instance of a named Daimler bus model. It was available with Daimler 10.6-litre CD650 engine, in

Right:

Daimler introduced an under-floor-engined single-deck model, called the Freeline, in 1951. The second such chassis, number 25001, was delivered to Duple in April 1951 to receive a metal-framed two-door bus body designed to carry 60 passengers, with half of that number standing — a concept then arousing some interest. Registered LRW 377, it became a demonstrator, operating for a time in Edinburgh and visiting other municipal fleets, with little success in attracting business, before being sold to Samuel Ledgard of Leeds in July 1956, whereupon its seating capacity was increased to 36. *R. F. Mack*

Above:

The Freeline's biggest user proved to be in New Zealand, where the Auckland Transport Board placed an order for 90 of the D650HS model with Daimler 10.6-litre engine. The first of these (chassis 25081), complete with Saunders-Roe 44-seat body, was shipped in November 1952, entering service as No 151 but soon being renumbered 201, as seen here. The remainder of the batch had similar bodies exported as 'completely knocked-down' kits of parts for local assembly; 70 more followed in 1956-8. *IAL*

Right:

Scarborough Bus Service, of Perth, Australia, placed this Freeline D650H (chassis 25049) in service in 1953. The body, built in its own workshops, seated 48 — note the use of the 'eyebrows' motif as by then standard on CV-series double-deckers. This operator built up a fleet of nine Freeline buses; in 1968 this bus and some others from the Scarborough fleet, by then acquired by Metropolitan Transport Trust, Perth, were rebodied, in this case by Boltons. *IAL*

Above

The Freeline chassis was similar in design to other underfloor-engined models of the early 1950s in having a relatively high straight frame with the engine slung beneath it. Shown is a 1954 example of the 20ft 4in-wheelbase version then newly introduced as an option to the 17ft 6in and 16ft 4in wheelbase lengths (the latter for home-market models); a G6HS model with Gardner engine, it seems likely to have been one of 19 of the long version for Johannesburg (25328-46). *IAL*

British municipalities, normally the mainstay of Daimler's bus business, were unenthusiastic about the Freeline — Swindon Corporation's four D650H models of early 1954 remained the largest municipal fleet of the type until almost the end of production. The reason for their purchase was the Whitehouse Road railway bridge visible in this view of No 82 (KHR 782), on chassis 25261. Park Royal built the centre-entrance bodywork, which had seats for 34 passengers and standing space for 26. *IAL*

which case the chassis type was D650HS, as on the first chassis, numbered 25000, which went for bodying as a coach by Burlingham in March 1951, being later registered for demonstration as LKV 218. The second chassis, 25001, was of type G6HS, having a Gardner 6HLW engine (the horizontal version of the 6LW), and went to Duple for bodying as a two-door 'standee' single-decker, registered LRW 377. This latter, exhibited at the 1951 Scottish Show, was painted in Edinburgh livery, though owned by Daimler, and began a period of demonstration in that city, where the recently-appointed General Manager, Moris Little, was then an advocate of single-deckers with high standing capacity.

In Britain, sales of the Freeline proved sluggish, but were saved from disaster by about 50 going to independent operators as coaches in the period up to 1955, the D650HS reputedly giving very refined running. The lack of interest among municipalities up to that point must have been embarrassing, with only the 1952 Show example for SHMD, one each for Glasgow and Cleethorpes in 1953, four for Swindon in 1954 and another for Cleethorpes in 1955. Factors against the design were the power-hydraulic brake system (although an air-pressure option was quietly introduced from 1952) and the weight; by 1953 there had been a pronounced swing to lighter underfloor-engined models — notably the Leyland Tiger Cub and AEC Reliance — in the general search for economy, and Daimler had no suitable model to offer.

Fortunately, the Freeline received a warmer reception in New Zealand, where the Auckland Transport Board became the largest user, receiving 90 of the D650HS, placed in service in 1952-4, and then a repeat order for 70 in 1956-8. Indeed, the Freeline proved to be very much an export model, with 558 of the total production of 650 exported, the majority being the D650HS version. The continent receiving the largest total proved to be Africa with 203, including several municipalities and other concerns in South Africa, such as South African Railways, plus 22 for J. N. Zarpas, of Nigeria, a Daimler customer going back to COG5 days. There were also 108 exports to European countries, including Norway, Belgium, Spain and Portugal, while others went to Australia, Israel and India, where Bombay followed tradition with Gardner

Left:
The Freeline had slightly more success as a coach in Britain, mostly with independent operators, but when Coventry Corporation wanted three 41-seat coaches for its private hire department it naturally turned to the home team, taking G6HS chassis and Willowbrook bodywork, delivered in May 1959. They are seen lined up in Allesley Hall Drive in company with one of the CVD6 Brush-bodied single-deckers of 1949 which had been rehabilitated for similar duty. Note the white-coated drivers. *TWM*

Above:
Despite the efforts put into new models, the CVG6 continued to be the most successful Daimler bus model, by 1954 redesigned using the 16ft 4in frame and with features such as the gate-type preselector control first seen on the CD650. This photograph issued in February 1955 shows four on the production line, and accompanied an announcement that 75 such chassis had been ordered by British municipalities in the first six weeks of the year; bus orders orders were becoming more difficult to obtain than in the early postwar years. *IAL*

Above:
West Bromwich Corporation took delivery of 10 CVG6 buses with Metro-Cammell Orion bodywork early in 1955. Leading this scene at the depot is 183 (KEA 183) on chassis 18625, followed by 184 and 181 of the same batch. Partly visible on the right is

No 74 (AEA 4) of the original tram-replacement fleet of COG6 buses delivered in 1939. West Bromwich offered the lowest fares in the West Midlands, yet its fleet, in the distinctive livery of two shades of blue and straw, achieved a high standard of turnout.
IAL

Left:
The development of glassfibre-reinforced plastics opened up fresh possibilities for front-end styling. Daimler and Manchester Corporation co-operated on this design for the CVG6; the chassis shown, displayed at the Scottish Show in November 1957, was almost certainly an early one from the 19270-99 batch for that fleet which entered service from May 1958 as 4550 (TNA 550) upwards. No doubt Daimler welcomed the creation of a more distinctive style not used on other makes of chassis, although it proved necessary to make it in two versions — one widened at the base to suit the wider frame of the recently-introduced 30ft CV-series models.
R. Marshall collection

five-cylinder examples. In Britain the model had been all but forgotten by the later 1950s apart from three G6HS coaches for Coventry in 1959 and examples for Daimler stalwarts Tailby & George and Burwell & District, until, right at the end of production, Great Yarmouth Corporation took eight G6HS with dual-purpose Roe bodies in 1962-4.

At management level, Sir Bernard Docker's era as Chairman ended in 1956. He had married in 1949 and a series of very elaborate cars designed to meet the wishes of Lady Docker had appeared at successive Motor Shows, making her a nationally-known personality. On a more practical level, she is said to have influenced the introduction of the Daimler Conquest, a 2.5-litre saloon, imaginatively priced at £1,066, to broaden Daimler's appeal and meeting with some success. Sir Bernard was succeeded by Jack Sangster, who had come to BSA from the motor-cycle world, and brought in Edward Turner to take overall charge of group vehicle development.

Meanwhile, the CVG6 continued to be the mainstay of Daimler bus output. A fresh line of development was signalled by a demonstrator on chassis 18954 built for

the 1955 Scottish Show, its Willowbrook body being built directly on the chassis without the usual underframe, reducing its 'highbridge' body to an overall height of about 14ft; it was registered SDU 711. Walsall Corporation took 15 similar buses early in 1956.

The permissible length for two-axle double-deckers was increased to 30ft from 1 July 1956, and a new CVG6-30 model was introduced to suit, also available with the CD650 engine, in which case, rather surprisingly, the chassis became the CVD650-30. The prototype chassis, of the latter type, was on the Daimler stand at the 1956 Show, appropriately numbered 30000. It had been decided to offer it only in

8ft-wide form, and this allowed the parallel-sided frame, with no inward taper towards the front, to be adopted, with benefit to stability — this feature was copied about four years later by AEC on the Regent V. Air-pressure brakes were standard. Further work was done on both the CD650 and CD6 engines, including a turbocharged version of the latter, but double-deckers so powered were very rare among the overwhelming majority with Gardner engines.

Chassis 30001 was a CVG6-30 which received a 'low-highbridge' Willowbrook body in 1957 and became a demonstrator, registered VKV 99; in 1958 this became the first bus to receive a Gardner 6LX engine, which was fitted in place of its original 6LW. The 6LX was a new design, outwardly quite similar to the 6LW but increased to 10.45-litre swept volume by increasing the bore size to $4\frac{3}{4}$in, and giving an output of 150bhp, still at the conservative 1,700rpm favoured by its manufacturer since 1931. This engine would play an important part in later Daimler bus history (much as the 5LW did in the 1930s), although mainly in a quite different chassis.

Further fresh developments were in transmission designs, the Daimatic gearbox appearing at the 1957 Scottish Show. This was based on a Wilson-type epicyclic gear set and was equivalent to the Self-Changing Gears design as adopted in 1954 by Leyland for its Pneumocyclic and by AEC for its Monocontrol. It allowed direct selection of the gears by a miniature gear lever switch unit mounted on the steering column, the 'clutch' or, more correctly, gear-changing pedal being eliminated; it could also be adapted to give automatic control, and was at first offered as an option to the preselective type on CV-series models with air-pressure brakes. However, the Daimatic was designed independently by Daimler, including some departures from the Wilson design in regard to the brake-bands, destined to give trouble in later years. Some centrifugal clutch installations were also made in the search for fuel economy but, as applied elsewhere, harsh action and increased gear-box noise discouraged further development.

A further stage in the gradually changing appearance of Daimler front-engined bus models also emerged at the 1957 Show, when what became known as the 'Manchester front' was introduced — it had been developed jointly with that undertaking and was fitted to 30 CVG6 then being supplied — to give better engine access and close-range nearside vision, the front cowl being slightly narrower and no longer including the headlamps. This design had to be produced in two versions, to suit both narrow and wide frames, but became standard almost immediately.

A new and quite startling option was a David Brown synchromesh gearbox — the first use of a conventional clutch and gearbox transmission on a Daimler bus since 1931 — introduced to appeal to operators which still considered fluid transmission 'wasteful'. Such models, which had the wider chassis frame regardless of length, were designated CSG6 etc. They sold in limited numbers from 1959, early examples including six CSG6 for Cardiff, six CSG6-30 for Leicester and 10 of the latter for the independent Lancashire United fleet.

Early sales of the CVG6-30 were quite modest, the first bulk orders being for seven for Bolton in 1958 and a dozen for West Bromwich in 1958-9, but when the version with the 6LX engine went into production in 1959 as the CVG6LX-30, Leeds City Transport placed an order for 30; a total of 85 of the various 30ft CV models had been reached by the end of 1960.

Quite a number of operators opted to continue with 27ft double-deckers in the late 1950s, and such buses still formed the greater part of Daimler bus output, at around 200 of the 250 or so annual total. This was a lower rate of production than had applied at any time since the mid-1930s, except for the period of disruption caused by the air raid damage of 1940-1, and, although a drop from the strong early postwar demand was inevitable, the firm's position, with car sales also down as compared to earlier times, was becoming more vulnerable.

Below left:
Also at the 1958 Show was this front-engined CVD650-220 chassis, a development of the CD650 in single-deck 22ft-wheel-base form for 36ft body length. It had air-pressure brakes and the Daimatic gearbox with electro-pneumatic control introduced the previous year. Numbered 30024 in the same series as the 30ft CV-series double-deckers, it was later fitted with a Gardner 6LX engine and sold to Golden Arrow Bus Service, Cape Town, receiving a Bus Bodies (South Africa) 55-seat body. *IAL*

Above:
Leicester Corporation 182 (UJF 182), on chassis 30042, was one of six CSG6-30 buses with the David Brown synchromesh gearbox and Metro-Cammell 74-seat bodywork delivered in July-August 1959. The CSG models proved to be rare types, with only 17 examples of this 30ft-long version produced (all dating from 1959), although there were 18 of the 27ft CSG6 and five CSG5 built up to 1962. *TWM*

Left:
Glasgow Corporation had become an important customer, taking 195 CVG6 in 1954-9. One of the final batch of 45, with Alexander 61-seat bodywork, D237 (SGD 220), on chassis 19546, is seen on 15 March 1959 (its first day of service), operating on a former tram route. In August 1959 there followed five CVD6 with CD6 Mark VIII engines delivered with BSA turbochargers, although these latter were removed from two of the buses before they entered service. *Ian Maclean*

8. The Fleetline Success Story

Only 125 bus chassis left Daimler's Radford works in 1960, of which 60 were CVG5 for Kowloon and 53 CVG6 split between the Aberdeen, Derby, Manchester, Northampton, Swindon and West Bromwich municipal fleets. There was a contract to build Ferret armoured cars, an updated version of the wartime design, and this was to continue until the late 1960s. Car output was measured only in hundreds, with no medium-sized saloon to reach what had been the biggest market, although promising new V8 engines had been designed by Edward Turner and Cyril Simpson. Yet a couple of miles away in a former Daimler shadow factory at Browns Lane, Allesley, Jaguar Cars Ltd

Below:
There was just one CVD6 among the buses delivered in 1960, chassis 19661 having been built as one of 25 CVG6 models with Metro-Cammell Orion 60-seat bodywork for Coventry, the remainder of which were delivered in the latter part of 1959. It was fitted with one of the CD6 Mark VIII engines and was delivered in February 1960, being well-liked by the operator's engineers. However, Daimler decided to cease bus engine manufacture, and Coventry stayed with the CVG6 for its final batches of CV-series buses in 1961 and 1963. *TWM*

had a problem coping with demand for its cars, especially the new Mark 2 saloons introduced at the previous year's Motor Show; its total deliveries in 1960 amounted to 19,341.

The logic of the takeover of Daimler by Jaguar for £3.4 million agreed in June 1960 was inescapable and, bearing in mind that Sir William Lyons, Jaguar's Chairman, went into the deal primarily to gain factory capacity, closing down the bus business, in which he had no experience, might have seemed equally 'obvious'. Yet when he was briefed on a new model being prepared for the Commercial Motor Show that September, he decided it should go ahead and, as so often, his judgement proved well-founded.

The new model in question was the Fleetline double-decker, with transversely-mounted vertical rear engine, Daimatic gearbox and air-pressure brakes. At first glance, it looked like a straight copy of the Leyland Atlantean as introduced in production form two years earlier and by then selling well. This impression was reinforced by the adoption of identical main dimensions including the 16ft 3in wheelbase, long front overhang to allow the entrance to be opposite the driver, and the housing of the engine in a 'bustle'-style cover intended to project beyond the rear end

Left:
The first Fleetline, with chassis 60000, received the distinctive registration 7000 HP for demonstration duty. It was given a body built by Weymann and outwardly almost identical in style to those being built on Leyland Atlanteans, although the Fleetline's design permitted lower build while retaining a conventional internal layout. It had started as a 77-seater, but this was reduced to 72 for its spell with Birmingham City Transport as seen in this view dated 7 January 1961. This historic bus seemed set for a long and well-cared-for life after sale to Blue Bus Services in 1966, but was destroyed in a depot fire in January 1976. *A. A. Cooper/TWMC*

Above:
The first 10 Fleetlines to be added to Birmingham's fleet looked very like the prototype, whose body was itself built to a Birmingham-related specification. However, aside from being on CRG6LX chassis, they had bodies built by Metro-Cammell. The two members of the MCW bodybuilding organisation worked to largely common designs by that date, though construction in Birmingham was much preferred in those days of support for local industry. No 3248 (248 DOC) on chassis 60011, seen here in Edmund Street, was among the earliest delivered, in January 1962. *TWM*

Right
The Fleetline chassis
followed much the same
general layout and
dimensions as the Atlantean,
but its key feature was the
drop-centre rear axle. This
item was first seen on the
Bristol Lodekka in the early
1950s and had been adopted
for other front-engined
models, but the Fleetline
represented its first
application on a rear-engined
design, as exemplified by
this 1964 Show exhibit. *IAL*

Below:
The rear axle design allowed
the lower-saloon gangway to
run continuously from the
front entrance platform to the
rear of the lower saloon, as
seen in this interior of a
Sunderland Corporation
example with Roe bodywork
of 1962. *IAL*

of the lower saloon of the body. Yet this was done quite deliberately to allow bodybuilders to use similar structures, and the Fleetline was to prove very successful on the basis of its less obvious differences.

Cyril Simpson, who had been responsible for its design, had at first favoured a front-engined low-floor model. Bob Crouch, in charge of bus sales, had been intrigued by the possibilities of the rear-engined layout since seeing Fifth Avenue double-deckers of this type on a visit to New York in 1949, and it was he who won the day, but the Fleetline was also designed as a true low-floor model, differing from the Atlantean in having a drop-centre rear axle. The prototypes had CD6 engines in their final Mark VIII form, but by the time of the 1960 Show it had been agreed that the Gardner 6LX would be standard.

The Daimatic gearbox was mounted separately from the engine, thereby reducing the heat build-up that was often to plague the Atlantean to the extent of engine seizures. However, there was insufficient space for a conventional propeller shaft between the long engine and the gearbox, so a trailing-link coupling was used to allow for varying alignment. This proved liable to disintegrate when the engine sank out of line as its rubber mountings deteriorated (apt to mean a smashed transfer-box casing), and the Daimatic gearbox itself began to reveal some design weaknesses when running at up to 15 tons in the Fleetline. Yet these problems and some steering faults were accepted by most Fleetline operators because it was judged to be the best overall choice. In comparative trials the 6LX-engined Fleetline regularly used appreciably less fuel than the Atlantean, despite Leyland fitting its demonstrators with engines hand-built for efficiency.

It took a little while for the Fleetline to make its mark. The first chassis, numbered 60000, with CD6 engine as built, was at first briefly designated RE30 (signifying **R**ear-**E**ngined, **30**ft), and then CRD6 in more traditional style; it received a Weymann 77-seat body to the plain-looking style as already being built for the Atlantean and was completed in August 1960, being registered 7000 HP. It was in Birmingham colours and, having been fitted with a 6LX engine, went to that city for a spell at the end of the year before going on to general demonstration duty. Birmingham was the first major undertaking to place an order, for 10 similar-looking buses on CRG6LX chassis, to be used for comparative running against 10 Atlanteans and delivered in 1962. By the end of that year over 100 Fleetlines had been

Above:
As usual, Potteries Motor Traction took an early example of the new Daimler model — the CRG6LX chassis of the vehicle shown was numbered 60027 and went to Northern Counties for bodying on 27 December 1961. The bus became L899 (899 UEH) in the fleet, this publicity picture being posed in the following spring; the body was an early example of its builder's low-height design for the Fleetline. With the introduction of this new chassis, many other BET companies joined PMT as Daimler customers. *IAL*

Below:
Manchester Corporation placed its first 20 Fleetlines with 76-seat Metro-Cammell bodies in service in the winter of 1962-3 — 10 Atlanteans had been running since late 1959. Several municipal fleets were having difficulty in getting trade union acceptance of large-capacity buses, even though at that date all double-deckers were required to have conductors; Manchester's intake of new buses continued to include rear-entrance 65-seat CVG6 and PD2 buses until 1963-4. Fleetline 4606 (4606 NE) on chassis 60082 is seen whilst on loan to Liverpool Corporation in April 1963. *R. L. Wilson*

Above:
Midland Red's purchase of 50 Fleetlines was a major break with tradition, as most buses run by that operator — at the time, still officially the Birmingham & Midland Motor Omnibus Co Ltd — were BMMO models of its own manufacture. The Fleetlines had Alexander 77-seat bodywork to a modified version of that bodybuilder's standard style, using flat glass for the windscreens and upper-deck front windows. No 5274 (5274 HA) on chassis 60221 dating from April 1963 is seen in Meriden — the 'Heart of England'. *TWM*

Right:
Leeds City Transport was among the operators which decided to continue using front-engined double-deckers in the early 1960s. Most were of rear-entrance layout, but five out of 10 CVG6LX-30 models dating from 1962 were forward-entrance buses, having been purchased for use on the Leeds-Bradford service, worked jointly with Bradford Corporation, where this layout had become standard. As with most Leeds buses, Roe bodywork was fitted. No 575 (575 CNW), seen in the city in February 1969, was based on chassis 30144. *TWM*

Right:
Belfast Corporation followed a policy of having bodywork built in Northern Ireland whenever possible. For its first batch of 88 Fleetlines of 1962-3, the contract went to MH Cars Ltd, a business set up in Belfast by Myles Humphreys; the same applied to a repeat order for 63 which followed in 1963-4. By the time this photograph was taken in 1973, Citybus Ltd had taken over the Corporation fleet and 669 FZ, based on chassis 60672 and delivered from MH as No 669 in March 1964, had been renumbered 2669 and equipped for one-person operation. MH later became Potters (Belfast) Ltd and, from 1969, Alexander (Belfast). *IAL*

Below:
By the time this picture was taken in New Street in May 1966, Birmingham was back on stream as the biggest customer for Daimler buses, supply of the 300 Fleetlines ordered in 1962 having just been completed. No 3572 (BON 572C) on chassis 61333, about to make the turn into Corporation Street, had been delivered two months earlier, with the slightly less angular outline adopted for the later Metro-Cammell bodies in the contract. The bus following, 2781 (JOJ 781), a CVG6 with Crossley body, dated from July 1952. *IAL*

delivered, including batches for the Nottingham, Manchester, Belfast (part of an order for 88), Middlesbrough, Chesterfield and Sheffield municipalities, plus Lancashire United, some taking full advantage of the ability to reduce height to a 'lowbridge' 13ft 5in while having full-length step-free centre gangways on both decks.

An early landmark was an initial order from Midland Red for 50, delivered in 1963. That concern, then the largest company operator in Britain, had built most of its own buses since the 1920s, but equally significant was the appearance of several other BET companies among recipients of batches, early examples including Trent, Potteries, Tynemouth, North Western and Maidstone & District, all of the last three being unfamiliar names as Daimler customers. More were to follow and most customers soon placed repeat orders; Birmingham City Transport decided that the Fleetline was what it wanted, placing an initial bulk order for 300 to be delivered in batches of 100 per year from 1963 onwards.

Fleetline sales benefited from the upsurge in general demand because the big early postwar bus fleets were becoming due for replacement. The total of Fleetline chassis built passed the 1,000 mark in December 1964, and output began to catch up with that of the Atlantean. Most were basically standard 6LX-powered models, but a few users still favoured the Gardner 6LW engine and one of these, Walsall, requested special short versions, achieved by reducing the front overhang and moving the entrance behind the front axle; some of this type were also supplied to SHMD.

Although several CV-series customers soon switched to the Fleetline, output of the former, mainly the CVG6, continued and indeed began to increase — Coventry took 22 in 1961 and 25 in 1963, and Salford 36 in 1962, for example. The 30ft version began to attract export orders, with 70 for Kowloon in 1961-2 and 55 for Cape Town in 1965-6, as well as continuing demand from fleets such as Leeds, West Bromwich, Rotherham and Huddersfield.

A new variant of the front-engined range appeared towards the end of 1962 as a consequence of Jaguar's acquisition of Guy Motors following the latter's liquidation in 1961. It was decided to drop the David Brown synchromesh gearbox, which had given some reliability problems, and instead Guy's constant-mesh unit, as introduced on the Arab range in 1945, became the gear-stick option. Model designations for buses so fitted became CCG5 or CCG6, Burton and Darlington (formerly Guy customers) becoming customers for the former and South Shields switching to the CCG6 for 37 examples used to replace the town's trolleybus fleet in 1963-5.

Jaguar's takeover of Guy, which had quite an effective goods range, put a stop to a plan for Daimler to re-enter the goods vehicle market after an almost 40-year gap. Underlining his commitment to the commercial vehicle side of the business, Sir William Lyons had recruited Clifford Elliott, a former Dodge engineer, to design such a vehicle, and Elliott was now put in charge of engineering at Guy, supervising the new Big J range. Yet Daimler's drawing office was busy with another bus project. This was a rear-engined single-decker of the 36ft length by then permissible and numbered 36000, appearing at the 1962 Show. It and test chassis 36001 had a horizontal version of the CD6 engine set transversely, but this concept was not pursued further.

Instead, a design using a V6 engine was pursued, and one wonders whether the compactness of the vee-form engine might have come to Cyril Simpson's mind from his work on the Daimler V8 car engines, even though a bought-in unit, the newly-introduced Cummins V6-200, was chosen for what became the Roadliner bus and coach chassis, type SRC6. Cummins had a good reputation as a

Left:
Walsall Corporation continued to follow an unorthodox path under the guidance of General Manager R. Edgley Cox. A shortened version of the Fleetline was introduced, with the front overhang reduced and the entrance positioned just behind the front wheels. The production version, of which the first of 13 is seen here, was 27ft 6in long but had 70 seats; the Northern Counties body used curved glass at the front of both decks. No 2 (2272 DH) was based on chassis 60310 and dated from 1963. *R. J. Mallabon*

diesel engine manufacturer in the United States, mainly based on six-cylinder in-line engines too big for bus use in Britain at that time. The SRC6 was much simpler in layout than the Fleetline, with the engine mounted longitudinally but short enough, despite its 9.6-litre capacity and 192bhp output, to fit under the rearmost bench seat, driving through a Daimatic gearbox and a propeller shaft to a conventional spiral bevel axle. Air suspension was adopted, and Simpson had reason to retire with a sense of a final job neatly done. His successor as Chief Bus Engineer was Peter Windsor-Smith, who had joined the Jaguar group as a result of the acquisition in March 1963 of another (though very different) engine builder, Coventry-Climax, which, while specialising in fire pumps and fork-lift trucks, was famous for its racing car engines.

Chassis 36002 became a demonstrator bus but 36003 was bodied by Marshall to BET pattern for Potteries Motor Traction and, with left-hand-drive chassis 36004, was

Above:
Derby Corporation continued to favour the CVG6 in the early and mid-1960s. No 156 (BCH 156B) on chassis 20074 was one of 10 dating from 1964 with Roe 65-seat bodywork, as favoured in that fleet from 1961. It is seen during the 1970s in Derby bus station, recently the subject of local controversy, some citizens wishing to see it refurbished rather than demolished. *TWM*

Below:
The Roadliner SRC6 rear-engined chassis appeared to open up exciting possibilities. The Cummins V6 engine gave up to 192bhp yet was compact enough to fit under the rearmost seat, with the drive taken via fluid flywheel, Daimatic gearbox and propeller shaft directly forward to the rear axle. This was a display chassis (36105) exhibited at Shows in 1966-8. It had rubber suspension, optional to the standard air suspension — itself quite an advanced feature at the time. In this scene, sets of rear suspension assemblies for Jaguar cars can be seen in the background. *IAL*

Above:
The first Roadliner to be bodied, by Marshall as a 50-seat bus to contemporary BET Federation style, was exhibited at the 1964 Show and then placed in service with Potteries Motor Traction as its SN1000, registered 6000 EH. It is seen here in service in Newcastle-under-Lyme during the following winter. Initial reaction was good, not least among drivers — the local trade union branch even wrote an official letter of congratulation to Daimler, an unheard-of step. *IAL*

Below:
Another of the initial run of chassis was 36005, bodied by Duple as a 49-seat coach and registered CWK 641C for demonstration duty. The writer recalls an impressive day road-testing it, laden to the equivalent of a full passenger load for *Bus & Coach*, in which it climbed a 1 in 5 gradient and reached 72mph on a test circuit in a seemingly effortless way, giving no hint of the problems that were to beset the type in service. It was sold to local operator Red House Motor Services and is seen here in September 1975 in company with a WMPTE ex-Coventry Corporation Fleetline in that city's Pool Meadow bus station, the latter still much as built prewar, but in much-altered surroundings. *TWM*

Above:
The first batch of Roadliners to be delivered, in the summer of 1966, was of 10 for the West Riding Automobile Co Ltd, based at Wakefield — at that date an independent concern and perhaps then best-known for its fleet of Guy Wulfrunian double-deckers taken into stock in 1959-65. No 127 (FHL 820D) on chassis 36014 is seen on test before dispatch from Daimler; the 50-seat bodywork was by Plaxton. *TWMC*

Below:
For a time the Roadliner was regarded as a star model, and these two examples, both with Plaxton Panorama bodywork, took top awards at both the Blackpool and Brighton coach rallies. The Black & White Motorways coach, partly hidden here, was No 276 (KDD 276E) on chassis 36121 with 44-seat capacity, taking the Coach of the Year award at both events. Alongside it was London-based Evan Evans Tours' LAP 665E with 'executive' seating for 27, based on chassis 36158. The Mayor of Blackpool's car, FV 1, was a Daimler Majestic Major with V8 engine. *IAL*

exhibited at the 1964 Show. A Duple-bodied coach on chassis 36005, registered CWK 641C, was used for press road tests, and the author was among those much impressed with the lively performance and promising fuel economy. The engine had a typical vee-form 'wuffle', and indeed there was an inherent roughness because the vee angle was as chosen for an alternative V8 version, but this was barely evident within the vehicle, where the noise level was low.

Regular production of the Roadliner did not get underway until 1966, early deliveries including 10 for West Riding Automobile Co, 25 following an initial three for export to Edmonton, Canada and 24 for PMT. Part of the delay was caused by the collapse of a plan to build the Cummins V6-200 and a V8 equivalent in Britain, for which the Meadows concern in Wolverhampton had been acquired in late 1964. Jaguar-Cummins Ltd was formed but the plan was abandoned. Output increased a little in 1967-8, with 17 coaches for Black & White, following one at the 1966 Show, and 33 buses for Adelaide, but it soon became apparent that all was not well. Reports of unreliability began to spread — engines tightening up when hot and emitting excessive smoke were among the problems. PMT was the largest user, with 54 received by April 1968, but delivery of a further 10 on order was deferred.

Meanwhile, a double-deck application for the Cummins engine resulted from Daimler's response to a specification issued by Johannesburg Municipal Transport for a 36ft rear-engined double-decker, the model being designated CRC6-36. It could be described as a cross between a Fleetline and a Roadliner, much of the chassis, including the drop-centre rear axle, being an extended version of the former, but having the V6-200 engine at the rear, slightly offset to the right to allow room for a staircase at the rear as well as the front. The first chassis was completed in March 1967, being one of five with Allison automatic transmission (also used on some export Roadliners), followed by

eight with Daimatic. They were numbered in the Fleetline series as 62651-63, with a further three as 62890-2 completed in spring 1968, and shipped for bodying as 85-seaters by Bus Bodies (South Africa). The 36ft length limit legal in Britain since 1961 also applied to double-deckers but had not been taken up for lack of a suitable chassis, but Edgley Cox's swansong at Walsall was a similar CRC6-36 with Northern Counties 86-seat body exhibited at the 1968 Show. There had also been a few experimental Cummins V6 installations in basically standard Fleetline chassis, including the first, 60000 (7000 HP), in 1964, although when sold to Tailby & George in 1966 this had reverted to a 6LX.

A little earlier, the Fleetline had begun to appear in single-deck form, the first being 24 built in 1965 for Birmingham, based on virtually standard 30ft chassis, designated CRG6LX/SD, with 37-seat bodywork, to replace some front-engined 34-seat buses. A 33ft version of the Fleetline with 18ft 6in wheelbase appeared in 1966, in either double- or single-deck form, the latter, designated SRG6, being so arranged as to allow the rearmost seat to be mounted over the engine cover. The first user of the 33ft double-decker was Leeds City Transport, with chassis 61979, the first of a batch of 30 and displayed at the 1966 Show. Also at that Show was the first SRG6 single-decker of that length completed (61692), one of four for Grimsby-Cleethorpes.

Tacit admission that the Roadliner was in some difficulties was indicated by the introduction of a 36ft single-deck Fleetline, type SRG6-36, with longer front and rear overhangs, a demonstrator in Dundee colours appearing at the 1968 Show. At the rear, though not amidships, the frame was reinforced to cope with the concentration of weight at the extreme rear but, although this model was an effective answer to the Roadliner's mechanical problems, somewhat ironically it was to prove prone to stress problems in the structure not experienced with the Roadliner.

Left:
An alternative line of development was the Fleetline single-decker. Halifax Corporation's General Manager, Geoffrey Hilditch, saw the possibilities of a single-deck version of the 33ft model (type SRG6LX), for which Willowbrook produced 45-seat bodywork. No 107 (FJX 507E) on chassis 61442, was one of an initial batch of three dating from June 1967 — it is seen in Halifax town centre in August 1970, in the company of AEC Regent V and Leyland PD2 buses. *TWM*

Right:
The mid-1960s was a time of great variety. Representing a very traditional view of bus design was Burton Corporation. It had long been a Guy Arab user, but from 1963 had settled on the 27ft-long Daimler CCG5, with Gardner 5LW engine, Guy constant-mesh gearbox and Massey 61-seat rear-entrance bodywork; this model used the wide frame and hence the wider grille normally found on 30ft models. No 96 (GFA 96D) seen here was one of four delivered at the end of 1966 — the last three similar buses were delivered in January 1968. *TWM*

Above:
Among late customers for the CVG6-30 was Huddersfield. In this scene No 117 (EVH 117C), with Roe 70-seat forward-entrance bodywork on chassis 30321 dating from October 1965, passes No 459 (HVH 459D) with body by Neepsend to East Lancs design on 30398 of August 1966. The differing livery indicated that 117 was a Joint Committee bus — when it was new, ownership of individual buses was split between British Railways and the Corporation — while 459, with cream front, was directly owned by the Corporation, such buses inheriting the former trolleybus livery. *TWM*

Above:
The Scottish Bus Group began to swing to the Fleetline for its double-deck needs in the mid-1960s. For a while, Western SMT could lay claim to running the highest-capacity buses in the country, with a batch of 33ft 83-seaters. This one, R2137 (JAG 490F) on chassis 62331, had Alexander bodywork and was exhibited at the 1967 Scottish Show, its length emphasised by the low overall height of 13ft 5½in; the passenger boarding could walk to the rear of the lower deck without climbing any further step. Odd though it may now seem, most later Fleetlines did not take advantage of the low-floor capability of the chassis, a higher floorline being generally favoured because of the tidier internal layout, except where low overall height was essential. The unladen weight, at 8 tons 18cwt 1qr, was modest in relation to the size of the vehicle. *AATC*

Right:
Having put the shortest rear-engined double-deckers on the road, R. Edgley Cox couldn't resist having the longest for the Walsall Corporation fleet of which he was General Manager. Chassis type CRC6-36, with Cummins V6 engine, had been introduced to meet a Johannesburg specification for a 36ft double-decker and, as this length was by then legal in Britain, Walsall 56 (XDH 56G) on chassis 62852 was based on a similar chassis. Northern Counties built the rather austere-looking 86-seat 13ft 10in-high body, with doorways and stairs at both front and rear, which was at the 1968 Show in a non-standard blue-grey livery. It is seen on the Birmingham service in August 1970, being by then in West Midlands PTE ownership, but was little used thereafter and remained unique. *TWM*

Left:
Almost exactly contemporary with the Walsall
86-seater was the last batch of front-engined
Daimlers for service in Britain: five CVG6 with
Roe rear-entrance 59-seat bodywork for
Northampton Corporation, delivered on 1
October 1968. For this final batch, parallel-sided
chassis were used, and they thus had the wider
front cowl. The last of these, bearing the final
chassis number (20198) in the series that had
begun at 9000 in 1930, is seen here. Normal
operation of the type ceased in 1985 but this
vehicle was retained and is seen in January
1986. *L. J. Mather*

Another strand to the complex single-deck story concerns an order from CCFL, Lisbon (which was also receiving 40 Fleetline double-deckers), for 26 mid-engined
single-deckers, officially called Daimler CVU6LX, though
in fact these were Guy Victory models with Gardner 6HLX
engines and bearing Daimler badges because that name
was better known in Portugal.

Below:
Although the half-cab double-deck era ended in 1968 so far as
home-market Daimlers were concerned, the Kowloon Motor Bus
Co of Hong Kong had found that a new CVG6LX-34 version, with
extra length and heavy-duty axles, suited its needs. This scene
dating from about 1966 shows some of the first of these ready for
shipping, with temporary decking on which kits of body parts
supplied by Metal Sections were to be carried, together with
other models, including home-market CVG6s, Fleetlines and
Roadliners. Under the covers in the left background was a batch
of armoured cars. *IAL*

By 1966, home-market demand for the front-engined
bus models was falling away, although Huddersfield and
Bradford put final batches of 16 and 15 of the CVG6LX-30
into service that year, with Swindon, the last British customer for the type, receiving three (chassis 30447-9) in
July 1967; all these had forward-entrance bodies. The 27ft
model survived longer, and here the traditional rear-
entrance layout was found to the end on CVG6 batches
with Roe bodywork for Northampton and CCG5 with
Massey bodies for Burton. Finally, Northampton received
five CVG6, on chassis 20194-8, on 1 October 1968 —
these were not only the last front-engined home-market
Daimlers but also the last buses to have preselective gearboxes. Yet this was by no means the end of 'traditional'
Daimler bus production, as exports to Kowloon would
account for some 315 further CVG6LX-series models produced from 1969, the last chassis, 30764, leaving the
works in December 1971 — a creditable swansong to the

era of the half-cab double-decker. These were divided between 30ft models and the CVG6LX-34, of 21ft 6in wheelbase and 34ft 7in overall length, with passenger capacity of 118 or even more. This brought the total of 30ft and 34ft double-deck CV- and CS-series models to 750, the overall total of CV-family chassis built since 1945 being over 7,000.

Notwithstanding the success of its predecessor, the Fleetline double-decker was firmly established as Daimler's main bus product by the mid-1960s, and continuing to attract new users. Until then, the Scottish Bus Group had taken a conservative view on rear-engined models, tending to favour the front-engined Bristol Lodekka and Albion Lowlander, but 54 Fleetlines were added to the Western SMT fleet in 1965, Alexander (Midland) following suit in 1967 with an initial 20. What proved to be an even more significant order came from London Transport in 1965 — although for only eight largely-standard CRG6LX, forming the smallest group of several new types (including single-deckers) being tried, this was to prove the acorn from which a big oak tree would grow.

9. Into the Leyland Empire

Both the vehicle-manufacturing and bus-operating worlds were changing quite drastically in the late 1960s. The sequence of events at Radford began in a minor way in 1966 when the name of the bus-building part of the firm became Daimler Transport Vehicles Ltd in place of the 'back-to-front' Transport Vehicles (Daimler) Ltd. More significantly, the Jaguar group was merged that year with what was then called the British Motor Corporation, which was basically Austin, Morris and their offshoots, the result being called British Motor Holdings. Although this brought Daimler into a far larger combine, there was little direct effect on its activities, especially on the bus side, since BMC had no commercial vehicle involvement beyond medium-sized trucks.

The formation of the British Leyland Motor Corporation in May 1968 from BMH and the Leyland Motor

Below:
The creation of British Leyland in May 1968 brought the three principal manufacturers of city buses in Britain into one organisation. This picture, taken in Leeds in February 1969, is apt in showing a Daimler Fleetline in front of an AEC and a Leyland, for it had become the best-selling double-decker. All three buses belonged to Leeds City Transport, the Fleetline — No 151 (PUB 151G) — being one of 15 CRG6LX-33 with Roe 78-seat bodywork dating from November 1968; it had a relatively low chassis number (61999) because the first bus of the order was delivered in 1966. The buses following are a 1958 Regent V and a 1960 PD3A/2. *TWM*

Corporation was far more profound in its effects. Daimler had become Leyland's main rival in the bus world, since AEC had already been taken under Leyland's wing and no longer offered double-deckers. In one sense, Daimler was in a strong position, for the Fleetline was by then the top-selling double-deck model being produced anywhere, outselling the Atlantean. Yet Leyland was very much 'in charge', with Lord Stokes installed as Chairman of the new group, which had the backing of the Government, though not at that stage nationalised.

The Labour administration then in office had also decided to embark on major changes in the structure of the bus-operating industry. The Transport Act 1968 created the state-owned National Bus Company, which took over control of most of the major operating companies in England and Wales, the BET group's bus interests having been acquired and added to those of the Tilling group of companies, the latter under state ownership since 1948. The Tilling group had also included the Bristol bus-manufacturing concern which thus also came into the NBC empire, though a minority Leyland shareholding taken in 1965 enabled it to trade more widely and, incidentally, become a rival to Daimler in some markets. The Act also provided powers for the creation of Passenger Transport Executives, which took over municipal bus fleets in and around major cities.

The rationalisation of BET and Tilling policies took time, and, even after NBC came into being from January 1969, ex-BET companies continued their vehicle policies

Right:
The single-deck situation was proving more tricky. Darlington Corporation had previously followed a conservative bus policy, favouring 5LW-engined Guys and then switching to the Daimler CCG5 for double-deckers in 1964. On switching to 36ft single-deckers to allow one-person operation, it chose the Roadliner SRC6 for a dozen 47-seat buses with Roe bodywork, No 15 (MHN 315E) seen here being based on chassis 36108 and delivered in March 1967. Such was the trouble encountered with the Cummins V6 engines that, within a few months, a repeat order had been cancelled in favour of single-deck Fleetlines with Gardner 6LW engines — this despite Cummins' setting up a factory nearby to build smaller vee-form engines. *IAL*

An important new development was the one-man operation of double-deckers, which had only become legal in Britain in 1966 but by 1968 was being actively encouraged by the Government as a means of cutting costs. Ralph Bennett's appointment as General Manager of the Manchester City Transport undertaking fostered both this and new ideas on bus appearance. No 2085 (LNA 285G) on chassis 62698 was one of a batch of 47 CRG6LX-33 buses with Park Royal bodies to the undertaking's Mancunian design, this one dating from March 1969. *TWM*

The 36ft Fleetline single-decker was introduced at the 1968 Show, this example of the SRG6LX-36 appearing in Dundee colours on the Daimler stand. Alexander built the 45-seat body, the vehicle being registered as SDU 930G for demonstration duty. Although this proved a more reliable model than the Roadliner, the extended rear overhang with a ton of machinery at the extreme rear produced both structural and, to a degree, handling problems, the latter applying more especially when running empty. *IAL*

A final attempt to breathe fresh life into the Roadliner came with the installation of what was marketed as the British Leyland V8 engine, which was, in fact, AEC's last all-new engine design — it was a 12-litre unit which could give 247bhp, so performance was doubtless impressive. The prototype, chassis 36304, was exhibited at the Brussels Motor Show in January 1969, badged as a Guy Conquest (that make being better-known in Belgium), but is seen here under its true colours as prepared for the Scottish Show of November that year. *IAL*

much as before for a time. Although NBC was then firmly wedded to the Bristol RE single-decker, with 490 on order in the programme of deliveries for 1970, there was a brief upsurge of interest in the 36ft Fleetline single-decker, initial orders being followed by a total of 101 included in that programme, all going to ex-BET companies with Fleetline double-deckers already in service. The largest share, 71 after some reallocation, was for Northern General and its subsidiaries. There were also orders for 36ft Fleetline single-deckers from Belfast and Leeds, taking 30 each, and Dundee, with 25 in the 1969-70 period.

Despite these successes, the Daimler single-deck business continued to experience problems. An attempt to revitalise the Roadliner by offering the Perkins V8.510 engine as an option to the Cummins V6 was announced in August 1968. Black & White switched to the resulting SRP8 for 20 coaches in 1969-70, with a useful improvement in reliability, while PMT took its 10 outstanding buses in this form, yet further orders were lacking. There was one further stage of V8 development also begun in 1968, when the AEC-designed British Leyland V8 engine of 12.1-litre capacity was fitted in a Roadliner prototype chassis, designated SRL8, as well as in an experimental 36ft double-deck chassis, type CRL8-36. The SRL8 had one significant success in 1971 with an order for 27 for Pretoria, South Africa, delivered the following year. Even so, that proved to be the Roadliner's swansong, with 329 built, of which 140 had been exported.

The single-deck Fleetline did a little better, with 358, mostly completed in the period up to 1973. This total might have been almost doubled, as negotiations were in hand for the supply of up to 300 to replace Auckland Transport Board's fleet of Freeline models, then still giving good service. Then Leyland headquarters gave instructions that only the Leyland National, the integral-construction model by then in production at Workington, was to be offered. Auckland decided to give the subsequent order to Mercedes-Benz. The Leyland National was a joint venture with NBC, part of the agreement for which also put Bristol under Leyland management and, effectively, control.

Above:
Briefly, the 36ft Fleetline single-decker seemed to be building up quite a strong following, partly on the basis of wider use of buses of this size. Leeds City Transport 1208 (UNW 208H) on chassis 63377, dating from February 1970, was one of a batch of 30 with Park Royal bodywork. *AATC*

Below:
By the time of the Commercial Motor Show of September 1970, the decision to withdraw the Roadliner from production had become known (although one export order for the CRL8 version

was fulfilled in 1971), and the almost inevitable PMT exhibit on Daimler's stand was a Fleetline SRG6 single-decker with Alexander body, No 141 (later registered BEH 141H) being one of 21. Far more significant was the appearance of a Fleetline double-decker for London Transport — indeed two, that shown being DMS2, on chassis 63805, the second of the initial batch of 17, although by then the total on order had increased to 1,967. The roofline showed evidence of Ralph Bennett's ideas but the livery was all-over red rather than the adventurous style he had persuaded Manchester to adopt. *TWM*

Upper right:
Fleetline output continued to grow. Bradford Corporation was moving nearer to the end of the replacement of its trolleybus system (the last to survive in Britain), and ordered 40 Fleetline CRG6LX-33 with Alexander two-door bodywork, No 404 (PKW 404J), on chassis 64326, being seen here soon after entering service in August 1970. At that time Alexander was offering various styling options for its 'AL' body design, Bradford's choice being among the most angular, although looking quite imposing in its smart blue and primrose livery. *R. Johnson*

Lower right:
The Coventry municipal undertaking at first remained undisturbed when the West Midlands PTE was set up. Park Royal bodywork was chosen for one batch of 18 buses of 9.5-metre length, dating from September 1970. They had two-door layout with seating for 72 passengers, and were equipped for one-man operation — increasingly common by that date. This scene depicts No 63 (SWK 63J) on its first day in service; the single-decker in the background was one of a batch of Bristol RE models with ECW bodies dating from 1967. The Coventry fleet was taken over by the PTE as a consequence of local government reorganisation in April 1974. *TWM*

At home, the emphasis, certainly among city fleets, was back on double-deckers, not least because they could now be operated without a conductor, following revised regulations introduced in 1966. As it happened, the Fleetline had also formed the largest share of the NBC double-deck intake in the 1970 programme, at 123, with 59 of the then newly-introduced Bristol VRT and only 24 Leyland Atlantean. That was a transitional year and not representative of what was to follow, but Fleetlines continued to be supplied to several NBC fleets until 1972. Further north, the Scottish Bus Group switched back to Fleetlines after becoming disillusioned with the Bristol VRT, rather underlining the point by fitting some with ECW bodies of VRT pattern.

The first PTE to become active, in October 1969, was that of West Midlands, which took over the Birmingham, Walsall, West Bromwich and Wolverhampton undertakings. It inherited 737 Fleetlines, then the largest fleet in the country, largely from Birmingham, and WMPTE was to continue its policy, with regular orders for 200 or more at a time. None of the other PTEs was as strongly committed to the type, but SELNEC PTE, responsible for the Greater Manchester area (later taking that as its title), continued Manchester Corporation's policy of splitting most of its main orders between Atlantean and Fleetline. Elsewhere in the industry, the familiar municipal names continued to recur among Fleetline buyers — Belfast, Derby, Dundee and Swindon, to which others such as Leeds and Nottingham could now be added.

Added to this broadly-based success was London Trans-

port's decision to revert to a large-scale intake of double-deckers after briefly favouring wider use of single-deckers, adopting as its new standard type the Fleetline CRG6LXB, using the uprated 6LXB engine derived from the 6LX and giving up to 180bhp, with a fully-automatic version of the Daimatic transmission. The bodywork was to a style with clear echoes of Manchester's 'Mancunian' style as adopted by that undertaking's General Manager, Ralph Bennett, just before he left to become an LTE Board member, although with rather less adventurous livery; the body contracts were split between MCW and Park Royal. There were many minor chassis features to suit LTE preferences,

Upper right:
Among the more unusual Fleetline deliveries were a pair in the pale green livery of Harper Bros, of Heath Hayes, Staffordshire, delivered in April 1973, the chassis leaving Radford in December 1972. They were on CRL6 chassis, with Leyland O.680 engine, and had Eastern Coach Works bodywork built largely to the specification favoured for Fleetline chassis by the Scottish Bus Group, with the flat-glass windscreen by then obsolete for bodies of this general style as built in larger numbers on Bristol VRT chassis for NBC fleets. Seen here when almost new is No 34 (TRE 949L) on chassis number 67436. In 1974 Harper Bros sold out to Midland Red, and two further Fleetlines with ECW bodies were delivered direct to that fleet. *G. R. Mills*

Lower right:
The end of bus chassis production at Daimler's Radford works came on 11 October 1973. This sad scene shows the final chassis, the 7,224th Fleetline built, one of five for China Motor Bus of Hong Kong, posed at the end of the production line, leaving an empty assembly shop behind it. At the wheel was Bob Crouch, who had joined the firm as an apprentice in 1932, becoming Bus Sales Manager in the postwar years and without whose advocacy the Fleetline might not have existed; he was by then Deputy Bus Sales Manager for BLMC, and the Fleetline would continue in production at Leyland, but the best days had gone. *TWM*

the latter's engineers finding Daimler more responsive
than Leyland, but the basic design was accepted. The initial order, for delivery in 1969, was for 17 but there was
sufficient confidence, based partly on good experience
with the eight supplied in 1965, to order a further 100
before they arrived, and then 250 more. The first two
examples, DMS1 and 2 on chassis 63804/5, were displayed at the 1970 Earls Court Show, and the rest of these
first 367 chassis were completed by late 1971.

An extra chassis production line was laid down but
engine supply was again a factor in production rate. A
Leyland-engined version of the Fleetline, the CRL6, using
the Leyland 680 engine, of 11.1 litres and much as used on
contemporary Atlantean models, was introduced in 1970.
The 680 was less bulky than the Gardner and it proved
possible to fit a conventional jointed propeller shaft
between it and the gearbox. Though intended largely as a
means of expanding production — the next LTE order for
1,600 buses for delivery in 1972-4 was to have more
Leyland than Gardner engines — it meant that some
operators who had hitherto favoured Leyland buses were
also attracted. Southend Corporation took 26 CRL6 in
1971 and favoured the Leyland-engined Fleetline to the
end of production. In practice, the first 400 of the 1,600-
vehicle London order went through as 149 CRL6 and 251
CRG6 but the second such batch were all built as CRL6.

Sir William Lyons retired as Chairman and Chief Executive of Jaguar Cars Ltd in 1972. Aside from the success
of the cars (a record figure of 32,589, mainly XJ6, had
been delivered in 1971), he had the satisfaction of seeing
Daimler bus chassis production at Radford also running at
the highest level ever achieved. Deliveries of Fleetline
double-deckers to British operators reached 1,144 in 1973,

not far short of twice the 646 figure reached by the Leyland Atlantean, according to an analysis of PSV Circle
records made by Paul Heels for *The Omnibus Magazine*. In
some weeks, 28 chassis came off the line — a vastly
healthier position than that inherited when Jaguar took
over Daimler in 1960.

Lyons was succeeded by F. R. W. ('Lofty') England,
who had begun his career as a Daimler apprentice and
joined Jaguar as Service Manager in 1946. He was much
respected, but increasingly the key decisions were being
taken at Leyland. It was announced in 1973 that Daimler
bus production was to be moved to Leyland, ostensibly to
allow more space for production of the XJ models. In fact,
the space thus vacated at the Radford works was not filled
and, while this may have been because of later changes of
plan, it was symptomatic of a change of philosophy, with
output and indeed all elements of policy seen in overall
group terms rather than regarding each firm as a separate
business. Yet, on paper, there seemed no reason to doubt

that a move of production to another factory having a long
history of high-quality engineering should be successful.

The last Fleetline chassis built at Radford was 67993,
one of five for export to the China Motor Bus Co Ltd,
Hong Kong, and, logically, the highest-numbered bus
chassis to be built there. In fact, in usual Daimler fashion,
each order in hand had reached its own point in the chassis
number series; for example, the London CRL6 order had
reached 67144 at Coventry and the first Leyland-built
Fleetline was the continuation of this contract at 67145,
though London CRG6 chassis 67233-61 were Coventry-
built. The official total number of Fleetlines built at Radford was 7,224.

In theory, Leyland was to pick up the threads where
Radford had left off, and there was a brief period when
both factories were delivering chassis. This gave an
illusion of a smooth transfer, but the first 100 Leyland-
assembled chassis were based on kits of parts supplied
by Daimler. Problems began to arise when Leyland
began making Fleetline parts; doubtless it was logical to
rationalise methods but long delays built up. Most

embarrassingly, when bodied vehicles began reaching
operators, many soon failed in service with severe gearbox
slip, due to an unintentional change in the grooving of the
gearbox brake drums; however, this also showed up a more
fundamental failing in the Daimatic gearbox, never fully
overcome despite successive redesigns. Putting it right
involved extensive dismantling and many new buses were
put out of service until enough parts to the correct design
could be made available, this in turn causing more delay in
new production. It was unfortunate that this coincided with
the period when three-day working was imposed on manufacturers due to a fuel crisis.

Eventually, over a period extending to 1975 or in certain
cases 1976, what could be regarded as the Daimler series
of chassis numbers was topped up by 1,487 Leyland-built
chassis — the highest resulting chassis number was 68948.
In the insensitive way of the times, Leyland had decided
that the model would henceforth be called the Leyland
Fleetline and its type designation was also altered,
beginning with FE, signifying **F**leetline, followed by the
nominal length in feet — 30 or 33; A for air brakes; G or L
to indicate engine make, and R for right-hand drive — no
further left-hand-drive examples were built. No fundamental changes were made to what by then was quite an
old design, beyond power-assisted steering becoming
standard, and the altered designations seemed to many
operators to be a case of change for change's sake; by
contrast, the Atlantean, in moving from the PDR to the
AN68 series, had become a much-improved model. More
understandable was a switch to Leyland's seven-figure
chassis number system, beginning with 7500870, which
was actually a CRG6 for China Motor Bus — Hong Kong

Above:
By early 1974, London Transport's Fleetline deliveries had exceeded the 1,200 mark. Those with MCW bodies were numbered in a series from DMS1248 upwards; DMS1626 was based on a Leyland 680-engined CRL6 chassis (67224), in common with all LTE's 1974 Fleetline deliveries, and dated from February of that year. Chassis construction had switched to Leyland, this being an early example. *IAL*

Above:
London's Fleetline chassis incorporated various non-standard features, including the style of instrument panel seen on DMS1596, a CRL6 (chassis 67166). The bus is seen after withdrawal in November 1980, while with Ensign, the dealers at Grays, before sale to Graham of Paisley in February 1981.

The gear selection switch unit on the left of the picture was a product of CAV, makers of electrical and diesel equipment for commercial vehicles, and was common to AEC and other makes of chassis using electro-pneumatic control of Wilson-type epicyclic gearboxes. *Stephen Morris*

Right:
When a major fire destroyed most buses in the former Blue Bus depot at Willington in January 1976, the Derby municipal undertaking, which had acquired the business in 1973, was desperate for low-height double-deckers needed to run under a local low bridge. Three new Leyland-built Fleetline chassis with the latest type designation (FE30AGR) were sent to Alexander for low-height bodies to be built as quickly as possible, and these entered service in March. No 53 (NAL 53P) seen here was allocated Leyland chassis number 7600002. Note that it carried a Daimler badge, as continued to be the practice in various fleets. *D. J. Stanier*

Below:
Alexander (Midland) was also a recipient of low-height Alexander-bodied Fleetlines in 1976, MRF121 (SMS 121P), dating from May, being the first of 11 to enter service. These had Leyland-built CRG6 chassis completed in 1975. Their chassis numbers (67466-76) continued the series begun at Coventry, having been allocated when the order was confirmed, as per traditional Daimler practice. The previous number (67465) had been given to a Radford-built chassis for Alexander (Fife) delivered to the bodybuilders in May 1973 and exhibited at the 1973 Scottish Show in November as that fleet's FRF73 (XXA 373M). The picture, taken in Stirling, dates from August 1986, by which time the fleetname had become 'Midland Scottish'. *David Wayman*

Above:
SELNEC PTE had placed an order for some 350 Fleetline CRG6, to be fleet numbers 7151-7500 and for which chassis numbers 65659-66008 were allocated. Delivery of chassis began in 1972, the first 174 receiving L-suffix registrations, but after 240 were supplied in just over a year, production moved from Daimler to Leyland and then the undertaking was renamed Greater Manchester PTE. Delivery of the rest was not completed until 1976, 7484 seen here being the last with a P-suffix registration, the final 16 being R-suffix. Northern Counties supplied the body to the SELNEC/GMT standard design. *David Wayman*

Below:
London Transport had moved on to the B20 'quiet' version of the Fleetline FE30ALR for its last 400 Fleetlines, and DMS2395 (OJD 395R), seen here in Woolwich, illustrates the effect on the appearance of the rear end. The ducting on each side of the engine compartment provided inlet and outlet for ventilating air. This bus had Park Royal bodywork and entered service in April 1977. Small plates on the engine cover identify the model as a 'Leyland Fleetline'. Note the tram track still surviving a quarter of a century after the passing of London's trams. *L. D. S. Dolan*

Above:
West Midlands PTE's final Fleetline order was for 135 FE30AGR chassis with MCW bodywork, 6867 (TVP 867S), the second of the batch, being seen soon after entering service in the summer of 1978. They brought to an end a 44-year era of favour for chassis designed by Daimler, mostly with Gardner engines and, very often, bodywork built locally in the Metro-Cammell works, begun in 1934 by Birmingham City Transport. At 1 November 1978, the PTE's fleet was quoted as including 2,020 Daimler Fleetline double-deckers (at WMPTE, none were regarded as Leylands) out of the total fleet of 2,606 vehicles, with 65 further Fleetlines then yet to enter service. *TWM*

Right:
In London, although deliveries continued until August 1978, the Fleetline had fallen out of favour, and withdrawals had already begun. In contrast to the longevity still being demonstrated by earlier types of London bus, the model was by no means alone among more recent types in being discarded ahead of schedule. By the mid-1980s, only the final batch of 400 buses to B20 specification remained substantially intact; this view of D2545 (THX 545S) entering Parliament Square dates from May 1986 — the bus (chassis 7702243) had entered service in February 1978. *Ian Cowley*

was the main export market for Fleetlines, 786 examples being sent there new.

London Transport ordered 679 of the FE-series buses, completing its DMS/DM class, and bringing the combined total to 2,646. There were 140 FE30ALR and 139 FE30AGR, but the remaining 400 were of a new 'quiet' type with turbocharged Leyland 690 engine, given the Leyland project code B20 and designated FE30ALR Special. Deliveries were completed in 1978. Well before then, London Transport's early enthusiasm for the Fleetline, especially in Gardner-engined form, had cooled and disposals began that same year. At least part of the problem could be traced to an unwillingness to accept that such a bus, with its greater complexity and remoteness of the 'machinery' from the driver, needed more attention in the operating garages than its simpler front-engined predecessors, as well as calling for different overhaul methods. That organisation, though blessed with superb facilities at its central works, had succumbed to the type of bureaucracy which made it difficult to adopt the more flexible approach accepted elsewhere.

West Midlands PTE added 635 FE-series buses, mostly FE30AGR, to its existing fleet, the type remaining standard for that undertaking until 1979. Greater Manchester PTE took 240 FE30AGR, the last dating from 1980. Among municipalities, Derby and Swindon (the latter known as Thamesdown following the local authority changes of 1974) maintained a continuity of policy that could be traced back to the 1930s. The Scottish Bus Group took 118 FE30AGR buses in 1978-80.

Leyland had been planning a successor to all three of the group's rear-engined double-deck models — Atlantean, Fleetline and Bristol VRT — since the early 1970s. This proved a complex and lengthy process, but ultimately what became known as the Leyland Olympian emerged as the type which would take over general sales from all three. Accordingly, production of Fleetline chassis ceased in 1980, nominally the last being a pair of FE30ALR models for the South Notts Bus Co of Gotham, near Nottingham, a small-scale operator which had taken to Leyland-engined Fleetlines after earlier policy had favoured other Leyland-family types. They were bodied by ECW and delivered in

Left:
Some Fleetlines from the later
batches of FE30AGR chassis with
Northern Counties bodywork for
Cleveland Transit were held back,
with the result that this undertaking
was the last to place 'new' examples
of the model in service. Only 10 of
15 chassis built in 1978 entered
service with appropriate T-suffix
registrations in 1978-9, and,
although a further 12 with chassis
built in 1979 were put on the road
as V-registered buses in 1980, the
final order for 16 (also built as 1979
chassis) was again partially held
back, with only 13 buses delivered
with W and X registrations in 1980-1.
Among these was H147 (PEF 147X),
seen here soon after entering
service in August 1981. The balance
of three of the 1979 chassis and
the five outstanding from 1978 were
completed in 1982-3, the last of the
series, H157, being one of those
with a 1978 chassis. *G. K. Gillberry*

November 1981, although the last Fleetlines to enter service were four FE30AGR models for Cleveland Transit, not put on the road until January 1983.

In all, some 11,747 Fleetlines had been built since 1960. Although it is easy to link the troubled transfer of production to Leyland and London Transport's disenchantment with the model as not far short of a disaster, output had recovered quite strongly from the dark days of 1974, again taking the lead in sales of double-deckers in Britain until 1978 — home deliveries reached 678 in both 1976 and 1978, according to Paul Heels' analysis. Some 4,448 Fleetlines were produced at Leyland, which is a creditable figure against the much-improved Atlantean as well as fresh competition from other manufacturers. Despite London Transport's decision to sell its Fleetlines early, many of them then went on to have longer active lives with their second owners, some of which built up substantial fleets on finding what good value they offered; over 400 passed to major British fleets and over 350 to Hong Kong, some of the latter running into the 1990s. At the time of writing, Fleetlines (albeit Leyland-built) can still be seen running in a number of British towns (eg Halifax, Bournemouth, Swindon), serving as a reminder of Daimler's contribution to the history of transport in the twentieth century.

Left:
The last Fleetline chassis to be built,
in 1980, were a pair of FE30ALR
models for the South Notts Bus Co
of Gotham, near Nottingham.
Ironically, they received Eastern
Coach Works low-height bodies of
a style usually associated with the
Bristol VRT — the last on new
chassis of that design also — and
were delivered in November 1981.
Seen here in Loughborough in the
following September is No 116
(SCH 116X), which was on chassis
8002297; its twin, No 117, was the
last of all, on chassis 8002396.
G. H. F. Atkins